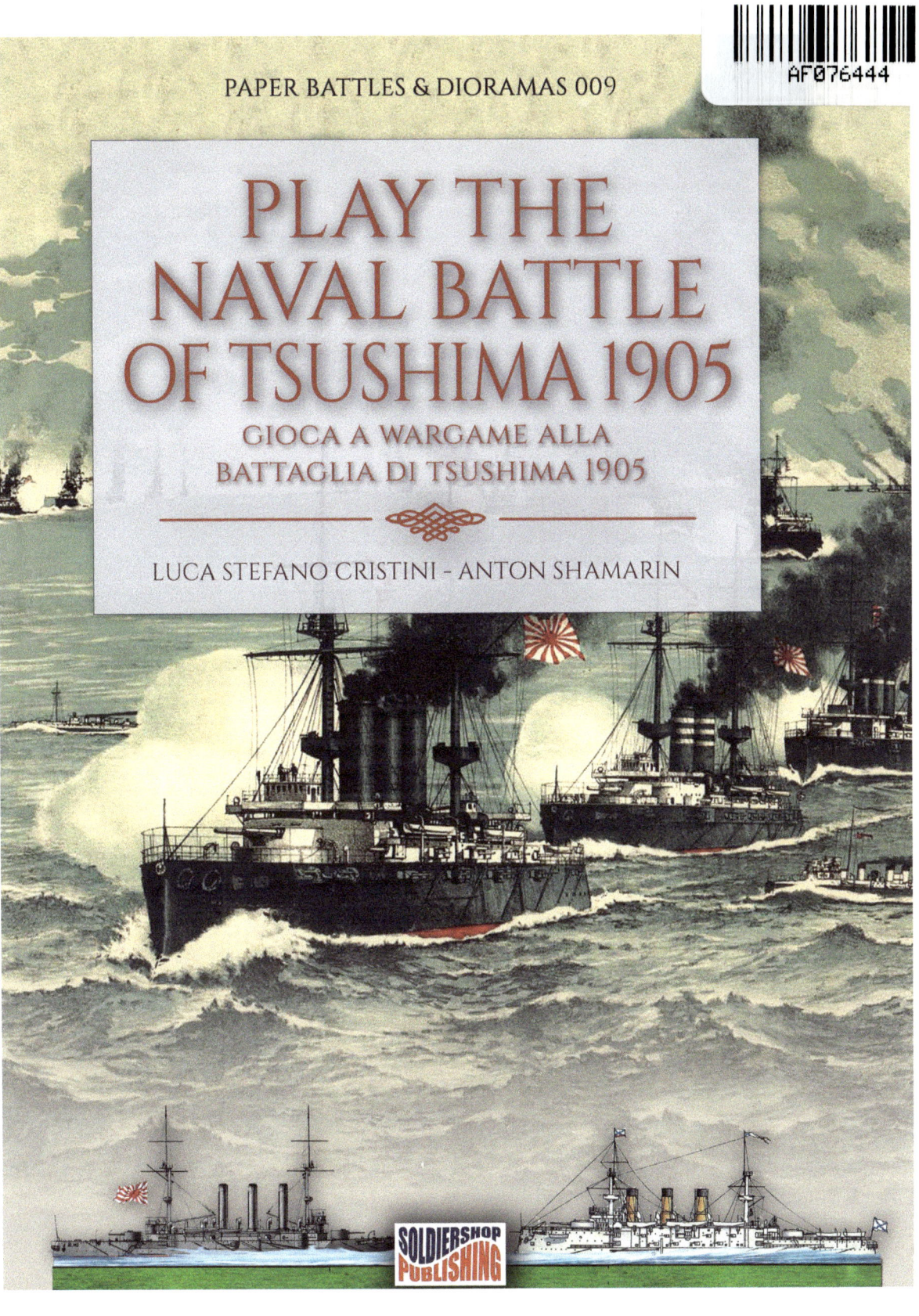

PAPER BATTLES & DIORAMAS 009

PLAY THE NAVAL BATTLE OF TSUSHIMA 1905

GIOCA A WARGAME ALLA BATTAGLIA DI TSUSHIMA 1905

LUCA STEFANO CRISTINI - ANTON SHAMARIN

SOLDIERSHOP PUBLISHING

AUTHORS

Luca Stefano Cristini has edited various publications on ancient and contemporary historical themes, including a great work on five volumes about the Thirty Years War and many others on Medieval and Napoleonic period, as well as several illustrated books with historical color photographs. He's also in charge for all the brands of Soldiershop Publishing.

Luca Stefano Cristini, storico e divulgatore da sempre di storia militare. Ha diretto per diversi anni riviste nazionali specializzate di carattere storico e uniformologico. Ha pubblicato un importante lavoro, recentemente ristampato su 5 volumi, dedicato alla Guerra dei 30 anni (1618-1648), il primo mai stampato in Italia sull'argomento. L'autore ha oggi al suo attivo molti titoli delle collane Soldiershop, Bookmoon e Museum sia in qualità di autore che di illustratore.

Anton Shamarin is a young Russian artist, expert in naval models. he is the author of most of the stylized naval models for our collection on the battle of Tshushima.

Anton Shamarin è un giovane artista russo, esperto di modelli navali, sua la gran parte dei modelli navali stilizzati per la nostra collezione sulla battaglia di Tshushima.

PUBLISHING'S NOTE

No part of our book may be reproduced in any format without the expressed written permission of Luca Cristini Editore (Soldiershop.com), other than for personal hobby use. The publisher remains at disposal of the possible having right for all the doubtful sources images or not identifies.

ACKNOWLEDGEMENT - RICONOSCIMENTI:

A special acknowledgement goes to our master paper kraft Giuseppe Cristini, expert author of all the "clippings" and assembly of our kits and buildings. We also thank GianPaolo Bistulfi for many of your finest flat figure of Russian and Japan soldiers and all the artists of flat painted soldiers not mentioned of the models belonging to the authors' collections.

Uno speciale riconoscimento va al nostro master paper kraft Giuseppe Cristini, esperto autore di tutti i "ritagli" e montaggi dei nostri kit ed edifici. Un ringraziamento speciale va anche a GianPaolo Bistulfi per averci fornito diverse immagini dei suoi "piatti" dipinti russi e giapponesi che abbiamo utilizzato nel libro. E poi anche a tutti gli autori di soldatini piatti dipinti non citati dei modelli appartenenti alle collezioni degli autori.

Title: **Play the naval battle of Tsushima 1905- Gioca a wargame alla battaglia di Tsushima 1905**
By Luca Stefano Cristini & Anton Shamarin
Serie Paper Battles&Dioramas edit by Luca S. Cristini. First edition by Soldiershop series. Ottobre 2020
Cover & Art Design: Luca S. Cristini. ISBN code: 978-88-93276627
Published by Luca Cristini Editore, via Orio 35/4- 24050 Zanica (BG) ITALY. www.soldiershop.com

PLAY THE NAVAL BATTLE OF THUSHIMA 1905
GIOCA A WARGAME ALLA BATTAGLIA DI TSUSHIMA 1905

PREFACE

An epic battle followed by an even more epic, absurd, very long journey that brought three Russian naval teams to their tragic fate. Circumnavigating Africa with a rendezvous in Madagascar, then sailing up the Indian Ocean, they rounded Singapore and after almost eight months they reached the fatal appointment with the Japanese fleet that was there waiting for them.

The Russian ships also had their merits, they were still the fifth fleet in the world, but the long voyage, the need to make numbers etc. and in particular that western arrogance in treating the Japanese like barbarians made the difference, and what a difference. The Japanese Admiral Togo had plenty of time to develop his already valuable fleet, superior in all respects, more modern, agile and much better conducted. The result was already written, in the biggest battle between battleships so far, the struggle was the slaughter of the Tsarist navy, very few Russian ships escaped the massacre.

Our book presents all the major units present at the battle, as well as many additional labels to complete practically both fleets. All you have to do is to wear the uniforms of Togo and the unfortunate Rozestvensky, his worthy adversary, who was well aware of the big problems his fleet would encounter.

Now you will know the developments of the historical battle and by doing it again, adopting tactics and attentions different from those that happened that distant day in May 1905, you will be able to lead the Russian fleet trying to somehow reverse the outcome of the story.

PREFAZIONE

Un'epica battaglia seguita ad un ancor più epico assurdo lunghissimo viaggio che portò ben tre squadre navali russe al loro tragico destino. Circumnavigando l'Africa con tappa d'incontro in Madagascar, per poi risalire tutto l'oceano Indiano, quindi doppiarono Singapore e dopo quasi otto mesi giunsero al fatale appuntamento con la flotta giapponese che era li ad aspettarli.

Le navi russe avevano anche dei pregi, erano pur sempre la quinta flotta mondiale, ma il lungo viaggio, l'esigenza di far numero ecc. e soprattutto quella arroganza occidentale di trattare i giapponesi alla stregua di barbari alla fine fecero la differenza, e che differenza. L'ammiraglio giapponese Togo ebbe tutto il tempo di mettere a punto la già validissima sua flotta, superiore sotto tutti i punti di vista, più moderna, e agile e assai meglio condotta. Il risultato era già scritto, nelle più grande battaglie fra corazzate fino a quel momento, la lotta fu l'ecatombe della marina zarista, pochissime furono le navi russe che scamparono al macello.

Il nostro libro presenta tutte le maggiori unità presenti allo scontro, ed anche moltissime etichette aggiuntive per completare praticamente tutte le due flotte. Non dovete far altro che vestire le uniformi di Togo e dello sfortunato Rozestvenskij suo degno avversario, il quale era ben conscio dei grossi problemi che la sua flotta avrebbe incontrato. Ora conoscerete gli sviluppi della storica battaglia e rifacendola, adottando tattiche e attenzioni diverse da quelle che accaddero quel lontano giorno di maggio del 1905, tentare se guiderete la flotta russa di invertire in qualche modo l'esito della storia.

HOW TO ASSEMBLE YOUR PAPER FLEETS AND YOUR DIORAMAS
COME MONTARE LE VOSTRE FLOTTE DI CARTA E I VOSTRI DIORAMI

In order to create the various ships of the two fleets, you can directly use our sheets, alternatively, photocopy them (only and exclusively for personal use, any other right is excluded). Our sheets have a size of 8x10 inches, (20.3 x 25.4 cm). the ships have an average size of 50mm by 85mm. If you want to get ships in different scale, you must either reduce them or, on the opposite, enlarge them in scale. We recommend using professional or service copiers that certainly offer better print quality. The bases that simulate the sea have a length of about 90mm and always show the name of the unit and the nation to which it belongs and also the specialty (ironclad, cruiser and so on). Our ship and paper soldier kits are generally easy to assemble.

We recommend using 80 or 100 grams of cardboard, not thicker otherwise you will have some difficulty when cutting, and that's the optimal weight once the glue dries. For what concerns the glue you have many possibilities, it just depends on your experiences, Vinylic, UHU or glue stick are always indicated. As you can see, our models are printed on both sides to obtain a superb result. Each group is generally divided by a thin line (or not) that indicates the exact position in which

Per favorire la creazione delle due flotte potete utilizzare direttamente i nostri fogli o in alternativa fotocopiarli (esclusivamente per uso personale, ogni altro diritto è escluso). I nostri fogli sono nel formato 8x10 pollici (20,3 cm x 25,4 cm). le navi hanno una dimensione media di 50mm per 85 mm. Se si vogliono ottenere navi in scala diversa da quella fornita basterà ridurre o ingrandire in scala. Consigliamo di utilizzare fotocopiatrici professionali, o service, che certamente offrono una migliore qualità di stampa. Le basi che simulano il mare hanno una lunghezza di circa 90mm e riportano sempre il nome della unità e della nazione cui appartiene e anche il tipo (corazzata, incrociatore ecc.) I nostri kit di navi e soldatini sono generalmente facili da montare. Consigliamo di utilizzare cartoncini di 150/200 grammi per metro, non più spessi altrimenti sarà più complicato tagliare tutto quanto, e in ogni caso quel peso è l'ideale una volta asciugata la colla. Per quanto riguarda il collante avete molte possibilità, Vinavil, UHU o colle stick sempre pratiche. I nostri modelli sono stampati su due lati per ottenere un risultato superbo. Ogni gruppo è generalmente diviso da una sottile linea o meno che indica la esatta po-

Paper sheets - I fogli coi modelli

Japanese Squadron Ironclad 1905 (15 Tons. 18 knots) 1st Sq.
Corazzate giapponesi 1905 (15 ton. 18 nodi di velocità) 1a sq.

Mikasa (1900)
Principal armament:
2 × twin 30,5 cm/45
Type 41 naval guns
14 × single QF 6 inch
/40 naval guns
Crew 836

Shikishima (1898)
Principal armament:
2 × twin 30,5 cm/45
Type 41 naval guns
14 × single QF 6 inch
/40 naval guns
Crew 741

Fuji (1896)
Principal armament:
2 × twin 30,5 cm/45
Type 41 naval guns
12 × single QF 6 inch
/40 naval guns
Crew 650

Squadron Ironclad Mikasa (flagship)

Squadron Ironclad Shikishima

Squadron Ironclad Fuji

the paper should be folded, perhaps with the help of a ruler, and then glued so to match the two parts, except the bases that should be folded 90 degrees outward. Once the glue is completely dry, weld the two semi-bases onto a heavier cardboard that gives the base its solidity.

Once the whole thing is fixed, we must proceed to cut the "white" parts that surround the models of ship or paper soldiers and their weapons or flags.

Use scissors or cutters for this, depending on the part you have to work with. Also remember to pay attention to the formation of units, following the instructions always given in the chapter of tactics or scenarios attached to the book. Additional labels with names of many other naval units are also provided in this book.

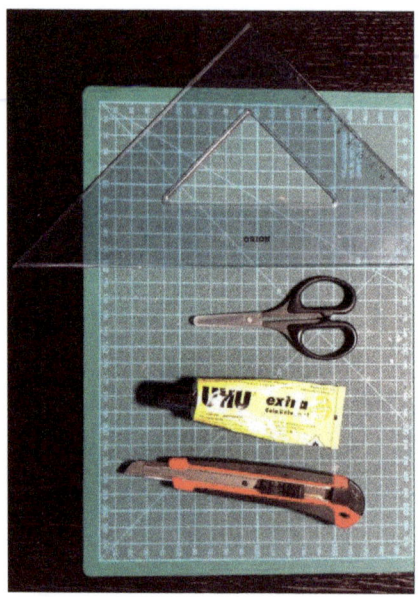

Tools & glue - Attrezzi e colla

sizione in cui la carta va piegata, magari aiutandosi con un righello, e poi incollata in modo da far combaciare le due parti, ad eccezione delle basi che invece vanno piegate di 90 gradi verso l'esterno. Una volta secca la colla saldiamo le due semi basi su un cartoncino più pesante per conferire solidità al modello finito. Una volta saldato il tutto, se volte potete anche procedere a tagliare le parti "bianche" che circondano i modelli navali e i soldatini. Oppure manteneteli cosi, titagliando solo il perimetro esterno. Utilizzate per questo lavoro forbici o cutter a seconda della pratica che avrete sviluppato. Ricordate anche di prestare attenzione alla formazione delle unità, seguendo le indicazioni fornite nel capitolo delle tattiche o degli scenari sempre allegati nel libro. In questo libro sono forniti anche etichette aggiuntive con nomi di molte altre unità navali.

▲ Japanese battleship (ironclad 16 Tons.) Asahi - *Bella foto della corazzata giapponese Asahi di 16 Tonn.*

Japanese Squadron Ironclad & Cruiser 1905 (15/7 Tons. 18/21 knots) 1st Sq.
Corazzate giapponesi 1905 (15 ton. 18 nodi di velocità) 1a sq.

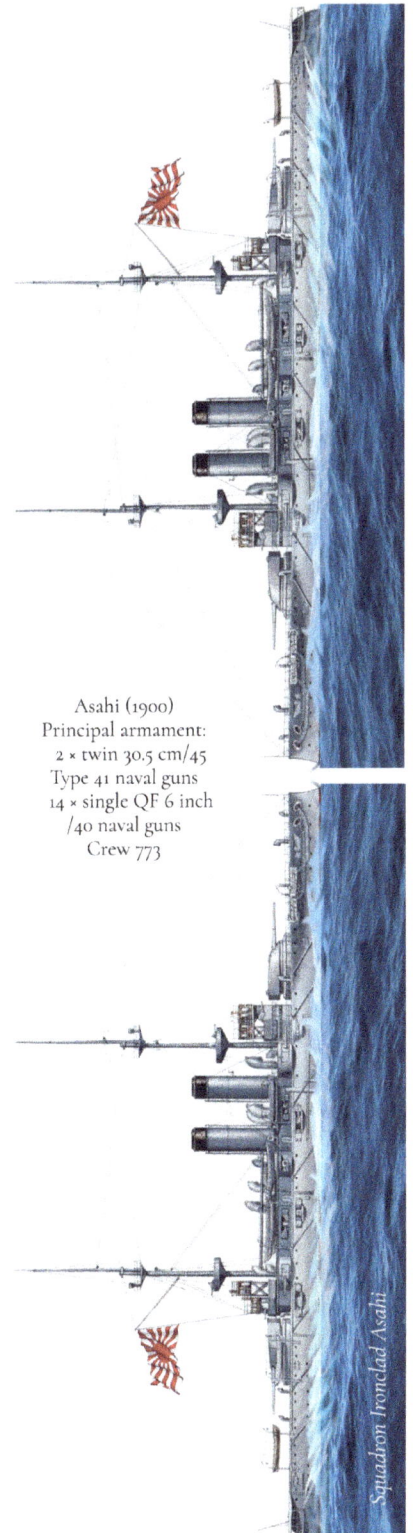

Asahi (1900)
Principal armament:
2 × twin 30.5 cm/45
Type 41 naval guns
14 × single QF 6 inch
/40 naval guns
Crew 773

Squadron Ironclad Asahi

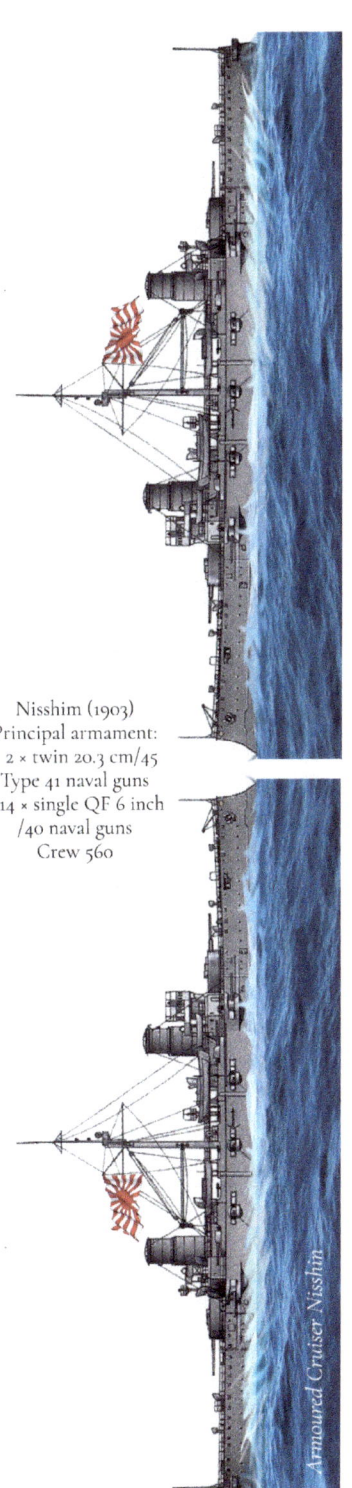

Nisshim (1903)
Principal armament:
2 × twin 20.3 cm/45
Type 41 naval guns
14 × single QF 6 inch
/40 naval guns
Crew 560

Armoured Cruiser Nisshin

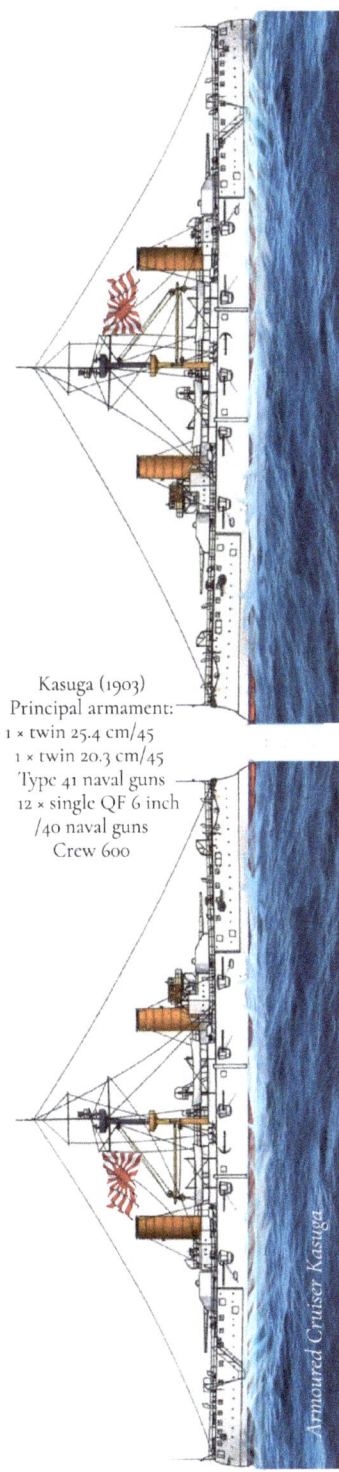

Kasuga (1903)
Principal armament:
1 × twin 25.4 cm/45
1 × twin 20.3 cm/45
Type 41 naval guns
12 × single QF 6 inch
/40 naval guns
Crew 600

Armoured Cruiser Kasuga

THE RUSSIAN-JAPONESE WAR 1904-1905
LA GUERRA RUSSO GIAPPONESE DEL 1904-1905

The Russian-Japanese War (1904-05) was provoked by rival imperialist ambitions of the Russian Empire and Japan in Manchuria and Korea. After unsuccessful diplomatic attempts, the Japanese, sure of the indirect support of the British and Americans, in February 1904 started the war without declaring it, according to their customs, attacking the Russian fleet in Port Arthur, obtaining a good success and forcing the Russians to take refuge in their base. This allowed them to control the sea and to transport their troops to Manchuria to assault the Russian fortress. The various attempts of the Russians to hold the enemy at the border failed one after the other and they were defeated repeatedly on the Yalu River, in Mudken and finally in Liaoyang (August 1904). The days of Port Arthur were now numbered and on 2 January 1905 the stronghold finally surrendered. The shame and thirst for Russian revenge led the Tsarist government to place all hope of revenge on their great European fleet. So in the end it was decided to send the Baltic Sea fleet to Asia under the command of Admiral Roscdiestvensky. But even this fleet was completely unprepared for a modern war. At the cost of

La guerra Russo Giapponese (1904-05) venne provocata dalle ambizioni imperialistiche rivali dell'Impero Russo e del Giappone nella Manciuria e in Corea. Dopo fallimentari tentativi per via diplomatica, i Giapponesi, sicuri dell'appoggio indiretto di inglesi e americani nel febbraio del 1904 iniziarono la guerra senza dichiararla, secondo i loro costumi, attaccando la flotta russa a Port Arthur, ottenendo un buon successo e costringendo i russi a rifugiarsi nella loro base. Questo fatto permise loro di controllare il mare e di poter trasportare le loro truppe in Manciuria per assalire la fortezza russa. I vari tentativi dei Russi di trattenere il nemico alla frontiera fallirono uno dopo l'altro ed essi vennero sconfitti ripetutamente sul fiume Yalu, a Mudken ed infine a Liaoyang (agosto 1904). Port Arthur aveva ormai i giorni contati e il 2 gennaio 1905 la piazzaforte capitolò definitivamente. L'onta e la sete di vendetta russa portò il governo zarista a puntare tutte le speranze di rivalsa sulla loro grande flotta europea. Così alla fine fu deciso di inviare in Asia la flotta del Mar Baltico sotto il comando dell'Ammiraglio Roscdiestvensky. Ma anche questa flotta era del tutto impreparata per una guerra moderna. A prezzo di innumerevoli fatiche e sacrifici la flotta

Japanese armoured Cruiser 1905 (9.700 Tons. 21 knots) 2nd Sq.
Incrociatori corazzati giapponesi 1905 (9,700 ton. 21 nodi di velocità) 2a sq.

Tokiwa (1898)
Principal armament:
2 × twin 20.3 cm/45
Type 41 naval guns
14 × single QF 6 inch
/40 naval guns
crew 676

Armored Cruiser Tokiwa

Asama (1898)
Principal armament:
2 × twin 20.3 cm/45
Type 41 naval guns
14 × single QF 6 inch
/40 naval guns
crew 676

Armored Cruiser Asama

Azuma (1899)
Principal armament:
2 × twin 20.3 cm/45
Type 41 naval guns
12 × single QF 6 inch
/40 naval guns
crew 670

Armored Cruiser Azuma

countless efforts and sacrifices, the fleet was able to make its very long voyage from the Baltic (see map) and with many difficulties managed to arrive, after almost a year of navigation, in the seas of eastern Japan. Here in the Strait of Tsushima it was surprised by the Japanese fleet that was waiting for it, and on May 27th almost the whole fleet was completely sunk. With the disappearance of the Russian fleet, the outcome of the conflict was decided. In spite of the military victories Japan was at the end of its forces both financially and in terms of military resources, while the Russians still had enormous resources to draw on and could continue the war for a very long time.

However, dangerous revolutionary uprisings had broken out in Russia and advised the Tsarist government to close down this humiliating adventure. With the peace treaty of Portsmouth (5 September 1905) Russia recognised the Japanese preponderance in Korea, gave Japan the lease on the Liaodong peninsula, with the bases of Dairen and Port Arthur, and the southern part of the island of Sachalin.

poté compiere il suo lunghissimo viaggio dal Baltico (vedi mappa) e con molte difficoltà riuscì ad arrivare, dopo quasi un anno di navigazione, nei mari del Giappone orientale. Qui nello stretto di Tsushima venne però sorpresa dalla flotta giapponese che la stava aspettando e il 27 maggio pressoché tutta la flotta fu completamente affondata. Con la scomparsa della flotta russa si decise quindi l'esito del conflitto. Malgrado le vittorie militari il Giappone era comunque allo stremo delle sue forze sia dal punto di vista finanziario che delle risorse militari, mentre i Russi potevano disporre ancora di enormi risorse cui attingere e poteva continuare la guerra ancor per moltissimo tempo. Tuttavia, in Russia erano scoppiati pericolosi moti rivoluzionari che consigliavano al governo zarista di chiudere questa umiliante avventura. Con il trattato di pace di Portsmouth (5 settembre 1905) la Russia riconosceva la preponderanza giapponese in Corea, cedeva al Giappone l'affitto sulla penisola del Liaodong, con le basi di Dairen e Port Arthur, e la parte meridionale dell'isola di Sachalin.

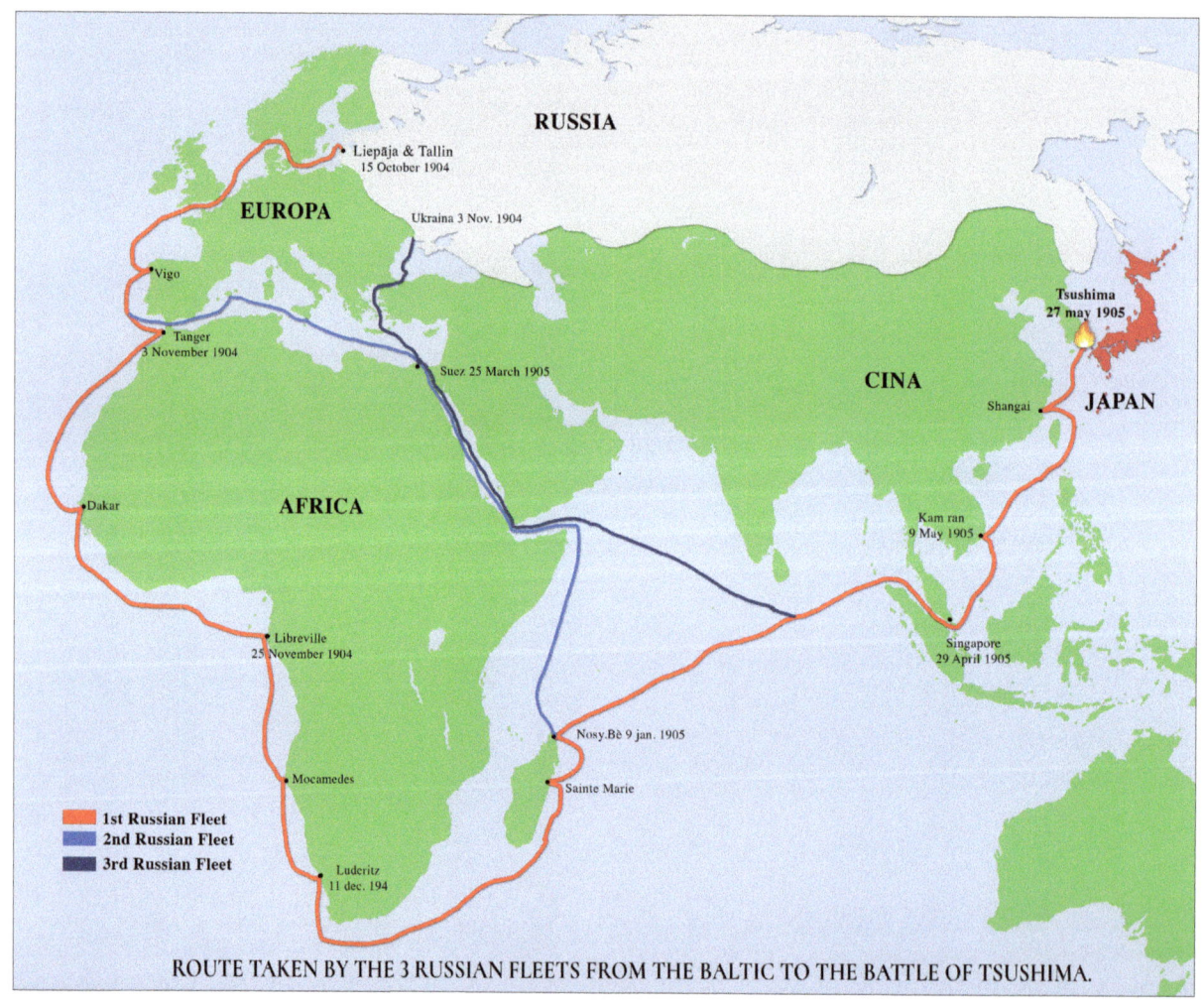

ROUTE TAKEN BY THE 3 RUSSIAN FLEETS FROM THE BALTIC TO THE BATTLE OF TSUSHIMA.

Japanese armoured Cruiser 1905 (9.700 Tons. 21 knots) 2nd Sq.
Incrociatori corazzati giapponesi 195 (9,700 ton. 21 nodi di velocità) 2a sq.

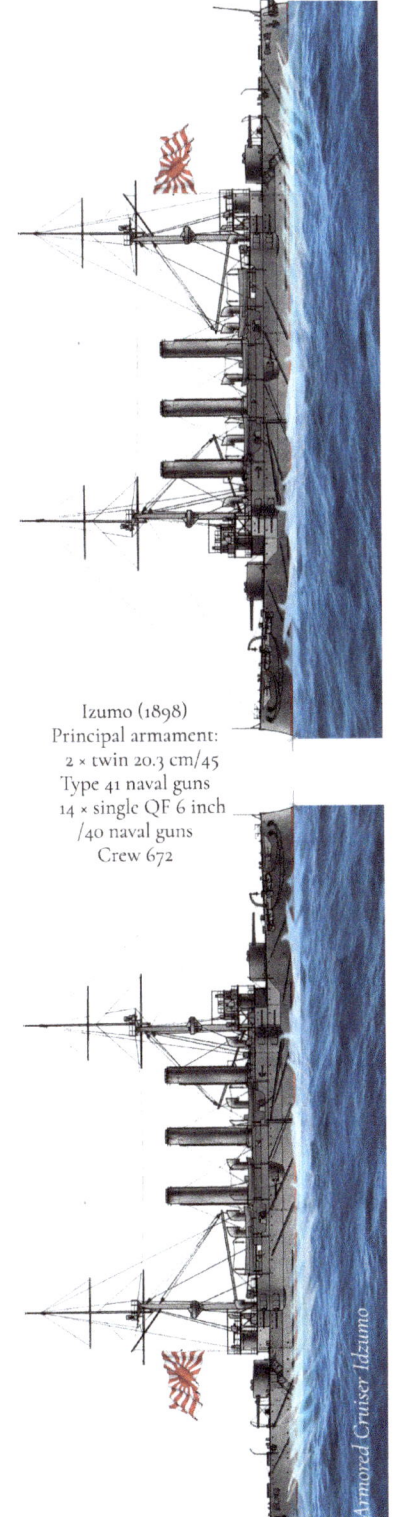

Izumo (1898)
Principal armament:
2 × twin 20.3 cm/45
Type 41 naval guns
14 × single QF 6 inch
/40 naval guns
Crew 672

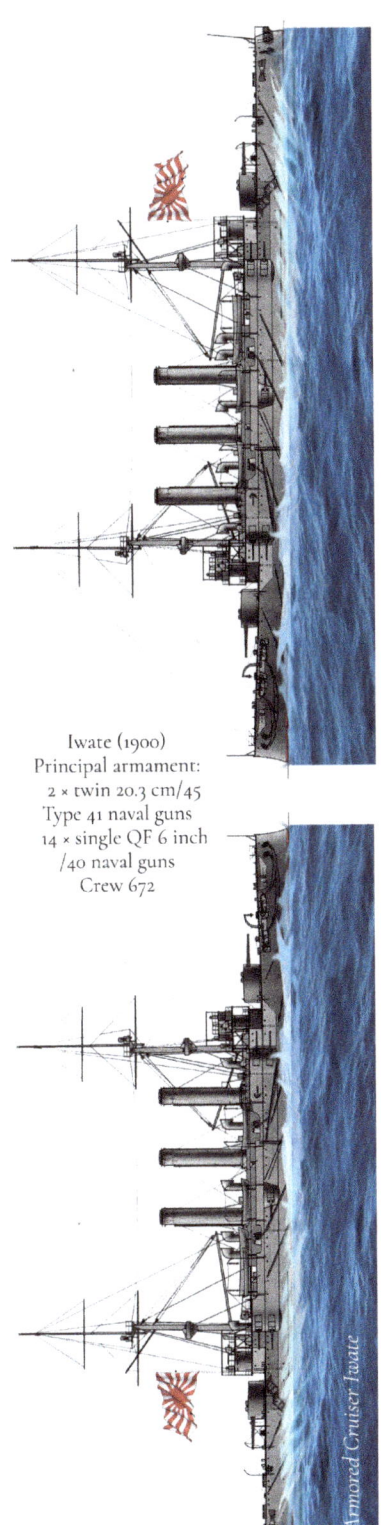

Iwate (1900)
Principal armament:
2 × twin 20.3 cm/45
Type 41 naval guns
14 × single QF 6 inch
/40 naval guns
Crew 672

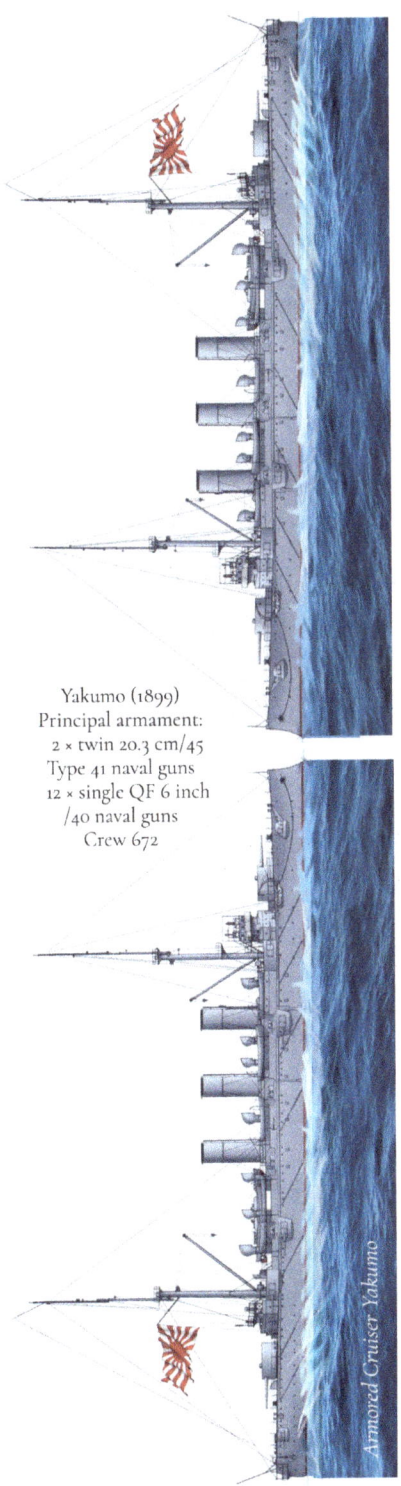

Yakumo (1899)
Principal armament:
2 × twin 20.3 cm/45
Type 41 naval guns
12 × single QF 6 inch
/40 naval guns
Crew 672

GAME RULES FOR 1905 NAVAL BATTLES
REGOLE DI GIOCO PER LA BATTAGLIA DI TSUSHIMA

Game sequence

1. Initiative stage: players roll a die. The player with the highest result has the initiative.
2. The player with the initiative moves his naval units
3. The player with the initiative fires his naval units or launches torpedoes
4. The second player moves his naval units
5. The second player fires with his naval units or launches torpedoes.

Movement

The ships can move at each turn at the maximum speed available to them, i.e. one centimetre for each node. See the relative chart. For the Russian fleet the old battleships are those in the table on pages 35 and 37, while the auxiliary cruisers are those on page 43.
For the Japanese fleet the slower cruisers are those on pages 17, 19 and 23. Each ship can make a 90 degree turn or less during its movement.

Gunfire

Any ship can fire at an enemy ship. Battleships have a range of 90 cm (36"). Armored battle cruisers fire at 80 cm

Sequenza di gioco

1. Fase di iniziativa: i giocatori tirano un dado. Il giocatore che ottiene il risultato più alto ha l'iniziativa.
2. Il giocatore con l'iniziativa muove le sue unità navali
3. Il giocatore con l'iniziativa fa fuoco con le sue unità navali o lancia siluri
4. Il secondo giocatore muove le sue unità navali
5. Il secondo giocatore fa fuoco con le sue unità navali o lancia siluri

Movimento

le navi possono muoversi ad ogni turno della massima velocità loro disponibile, cioè un centimetro per ogni nodo. Vedere la tabella relativa. Per la flotta russa le corazzate vecchie sono quelle nelle tavola a pag. 35 e 37, mentre gli incrociatori ausiliari sono quelli a pag. 43. Per la flotta giapponese gli incrociatori lenti sono quelli a pag. 17, 19 e 23. Ogni nave può compiere un giro di 90 gradi o meno durante il suo movimento.

Fuoco di cannoni

ogni nave può sparare contro una nave nemica. Le corazzate hanno una gittata di 90 cm (36"). Gli incrociatori corazzati da battaglia sparano a 80 cm (32"). Gli incrociatori

 Japanese Armoured and light Cruiser 1905 (5 Tons. 22 knots) 1st Sq.
incrociatori corazzati e leggeri giapponesi 1905 (5 ton. 22 nodi di velocità) 1a sq.

Kasagi (1898)
Principal armament:
2 × 20,3 10 single 12,0
12 single 76mm
Crew 405

Chitose (1899)
Principal armament:
2 × 20,3 10 single 12,0
12 single 76mm
Crew 405

Chiyoda (1890)
Principal armament:
10 single 120mm
Crew 350

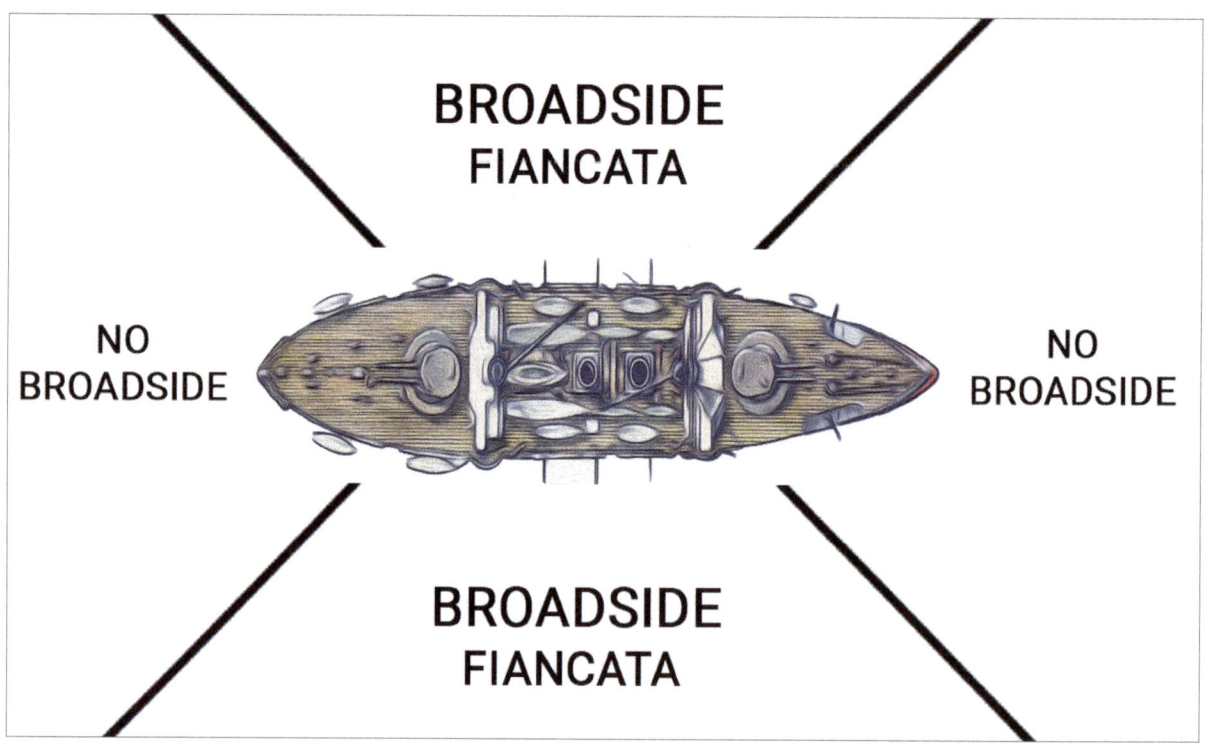

(32"). Auxiliary/light cruisers fire at 60 cm (23"). Destroyers and torpedo boats fire a torpedo at 30 cm (12"). The side of a ship is defined by 45 degree lines from every angle of the base (see image). When a battleship fires sideways (per side) it rolls 5 dice, battle cruisers roll 4 dice. Auxiliary or light cruisers roll 3 dice, fighters and torpedoes roll 2 dice. When firing in front or behind the Battleships they roll 2 dice, Cruisers roll 3 dice, Fighters and torpedoes always roll 3 dice. The ships get hits on the target for each shot of 5 or 6 at close range (less than 45 cm or 18"), or 6 at long range (up to 90 cm or 36").

Ships at sea block the line of sight for the purpose of firing, so you cannot fire if one of your ships stands between you and the enemy target ship further away. For ships firing torpedoes see next chapter.

Torpedoes

When a player has his turn to Initiative, he may choose to fire torpedoes instead of cannon fire. Offensive players making torpedo attacks select target ships and then roll 3 dice against each target ship. You cannot make more than one attack per target ship. Defending ships can roll the same number of dice. Compare the highest individual dice on each side. If the defender has the highest or even dice, the attack fails. If the attacker gets at least a six and the defender doesn't overrule it with another six the torpedo scores.

ausiliari/leggeri sparano a 60 cm (23"). Cacciatorpediniere e torpedo lanciano un siluro a 30 cm (12"). La fiancata di una nave è l'area a lato della nave ed è definita da linee a 45 gradi da ogni angolo della base (vedi immagine) Quando una corazzata spara lateralmente (per fiancata) tira 5 dadi, gli incrociatori da battaglia tirano 4 dadi. Gli ausiliari o gli incrociatori leggeri 3 dadi, i caccia e torpedo 2 dadi. Quando sparano davanti o dietro le Corazzate tirano 2 dadi, gli Incrociatori tirano un dado, Caccia e torpedo che lanciano siluri sempre tre dadi. Le navi ottengono colpi sul bersaglio per ogni tiro di 5 o 6 a distanza ravvicinata (meno di 45 cm o 18"), o di 6 a lunga distanza (fino a 90 cm o 36"). Le navi in mare bloccano la linea di vista allo scopo di sparare, quindi non puoi sparare se una vostra nave sta fra voi e la nave nemica-obiettivo più distante. Per le navi che lanciano siluri vedi capitolo seguente.

Siluri

Quando un giocatore ha il suo turno di Iniziativa, può scegliere di lanciare i siluri al posto di far fuoco coi cannoni. I giocatori offensivi che effettuano attacchi con siluri selezionano le navi bersaglio e poi tirano 3 dadi contro ciascuna nave bersaglio. Non si può fare più di un attacco per nave bersaglio. Le navi in difesa possono tirare lo stesso numero di dadi. Confronta i singoli dadi più alti di ciascun lato. Se il difensore ha il dado più alto o pari, l'attacco fallisce. Se l'attaccante ottiene almeno un sei e il difensore non lo annulla con un altro sei il siluro va a segno.

 Japanese light Cruiser 1905 (3,4 Tons. 20 knots) 1st & 2nd Sq.
Incrociatori leggeri giapponesi 1905 (3,4 ton. 20 nodi di velocità) 1a e 2a sq.

Niitaka (1902)
Principal armament:
6 single 152 e 10 76
Crew 290

Armoured Deck Cruiser Niitaka

Tsushima (1902)
Principal armament:
6 single 152 e 10 76
Crew 290

Armoured Deck Cruiser Tsushima

Otowa (1904)
Principal armament:
2 single 152 e 6 120
Crew 290

Armoured Deck Cruiser Otowa

Effect of Strikes

Battleships are eliminated when they receive five hits, battle cruisers are eliminated with three hits. Hunting and torpedo with two hits. The hits can be recorded on the base of the ships with small counters, or by marking them on a loss sheet. When a ship is eliminated it must roll a die. If the result is 1 - 3 it sinks, and is removed from the table. If the result is 4 - 6 the ship stays afloat (but abandoned and on fire) so it remains on the table and is an obstacle for movement and roll. Mark it with a cotton ball indicating fire and smoke.

Result

The player who has inflicted the most damage to the opposing fleet wins the match. You can decide whether to play on 16 rounds (equal to one day) or on 24 rounds by calculating half a day of the next day.

Bibliography

-Brown, David (1990). Warship Losses of World War Two. Arms and Armor Press.
-British Naval Attache Reports (2003) [1907]. The Russo-Japanese War 1904-1905. Nashville, TN: The Battery Press. .
-Busch, Noel F. (1969). The Emperor's Sword: Japan vs. Russia in the Battle of Tsushima. New York: Funk & Wagnall's.
-Campbell, N.J.M. (1978). Preston, Antony (ed.). "The Battle of Tsu-Shima". Warship. London: Conway Maritime Press.
- Forczyk, Robert (2009). Russian Battleship vs Japanese Battleship, Yellow Sea 1904–1905. Osprey.
- Friedman, Norman (2008). Naval Firepower; Battleship Guns and Gunnery in the Dreadnaught Era. Seaforth Publishing.
- Koenig, William (1977). Epic Sea Battles (2004 revised ed.). London: Octopus Publishing Group Ltd.

WEB resources

- https://www.youtube.com/watch?v=k__jr5uqjnA Battle of Tsushima (Empire of Japan vs Russian Empire) Reconstruction
-https://www.youtube.com/watch?v=ink4S1a-drhw&t=935s Naval Legends: Battle of Tsushima
-https://www.youtube.com/watch?v=kTm0eiwW4EY Japanese reconstruction.
- https://www.youtube.com/watch?v=jm4w2n1KjfQ Russian-Japanese war documentary.
- https://www.youtube.com/watch?v=y96_Pq6p4OI&t=10s la guerra russo giapponese (Italian)

Effetto dei Colpi

Le corazzate vengono eliminate quando ricevono cinque colpi, gli incrociatori da battaglia vengono eliminati con tre colpi. Caccia e torpedo con due colpi. I colpi possono essere registrati sulla base delle navi con dei piccoli contatori, oppure segnandoli di volta in volta su un foglio perdite. Quando una nave viene eliminata deve tirare un dado. Se il risultato è 1 - 3 affonda, e viene rimossa dal tavolo. Se il risultato è 4 - 6 la nave rimane a galla (ma abbandonato e in fiamme) quindi rimane sul tavolo ed è un ostacolo per il movimento e il tiro. Contrassegnatela con un batuffolo di cotone che indica fuoco e fumo.

Risultato

Vince lo scontro il giocatore che ha inflitto maggiori danni alla flotta avversaria. Potete decidere se giocare su 16 turni (pari ad un giorno) o su 24 calcolando anche mezza giornata del giorno dopo.

Bibliografia

-Frank Thiess, "Tsushima", Torino, Einaudi, 1937.
-Bonvi, L'uomo di Tsushima, serie Un uomo un'avventura, Cepim (ora Sergio Bonelli Editore), 1978.
-Richard Hough, "La flotta suicida", Bompiani Editore, Milano, 1959. (Titolo originale: "The fleet that had to die")
-Brown, David (1990). Warship Losses of World War Two. Arms and Armor Press.
-British Naval Attache Reports (2003) [1907]. The Russo-Japanese War 1904-1905. Nashville, TN: The Battery Press. .
-Busch, Noel F. (1969). The Emperor's Sword: Japan vs. Russia in the Battle of Tsushima. New York: Funk & Wagnall's.
- Forczyk, Robert (2009). Russian Battleship vs Japanese Battleship, Yellow Sea 1904–1905. Osprey.
- Friedman, Norman (2008). Naval Firepower; Battleship Guns and Gunnery in the Dreadnaught Era. Seaforth Publishing.

WEB resources

-https://www.youtube.com/watch?v=k__jr5uqjnA Battle of Tsushima (Empire of Japan vs Russian Empire) ricostruzione.
-https://www.youtube.com/watch?v=ink4S1a-drhw&t=935s Naval Legends: Battle of Tsushima
-https://www.youtube.com/watch?v=kTm0eiwW4EY ricostruzione giapponese
-https://www.youtube.com/watch?v=jm4w2n1KjfQ guerra russo giapponese documentario.
-https://www.youtube.com/watch?v=y96_Pq6p4OI&t=10s la guerra russo giapponese in italiano

 Japanese light Cruiser 1905 (3,4 Tons.19 knots) 2nd Sq.
Incrociatori leggeri giapponesi 1905 (3,4 ton. 19 nodi di velocità) 2a sq.

Izumi (1896)
Principal armament:
2 × 152 and 6 120
Crew 296

Naniwa (1885)
Principal armament:
2 single 260 & 6 152
Crew 325

acachiho (1885)
Principal armament:
2 single 260 & 6 152
Crew 325

Armoured Deck Cruiser Izumi

Armoured Deck Cruiser Naniwa

Armoured Deck Cruiser Tacachiho

WARGAME TABLES

Movements overview	
Ship Type	Movement
Ironclad	18cm (7")
Old Russian Ironclad and Japanese light crusier	17 cm (6,5")
Japanese Cruiser & Russian auxiliares ship	21 cm (8,5")
Russian cruiser	23 cm (9)
Russian Torpedo	26 cm (10)
Japanese Torpedo & Destroyer	30 cm (10)

Shooting range overview		Firing Dice	
Ship Type	Range	Broadside	Ahead/Rear
Ironclad	Just to 90 cm (36")	5	2
Cruiser	Just to 80 cm (32")	4	1
Light cruiser & auxiliaries	Just to 60 cm (23")	3	1
Torpedo & Destroyer	Just to 30 cm (12")	2	2

Gunnery table	Range	
Result	45 cm (18")	46-90 cm (19"-36")
Miss	1-4	1-5
Hit	5-6	6

Torpedo: attack and defense roll three dice, if the attack rolls a six and the defense does not, the torpedo hits. in case of a tie, the defender wins

Hits	
Ship Type	Success
Ironclad	5
Cruiser	3
Light cruiser & auxiliaries	2
Torpedo & Destroyer	2
Eliminated Ships:	
1 - 3 Sinks (remove)	
4 - 6 Burning (leave on table)	

 Japanese protected cruiser 1905 (4,3 Tons.17 knots) 3rdSq.
Incrociatori protetti giapponesi 1905 (4,3 ton. 17 nodi di velocità) 3a sq.

Itsukushima (1891)
Principal armament:
1 × 320mm and 11 47mm
Crew 360

Matsushima (1892)
Principal armament:
1 × 320mm and 12 47mm
Crew 360

Hashidate (1894)
Principal armament:
1 × 320mm and 11 47mm
Crew 360

TABELLE WARGAME

Movimento e velocità delle navi	
Tipo di nave	Movimento
Corazzata	18cm (7")
Vecchie corazzate russe e incrociatori leggeri giapponesi	17 cm (6,5")
Incrociatori giapponesi e navi ausliarie russe	21 cm (8,5")
Incrociatori russi	23 cm (9)
Torpediniere russe	26 cm (10)
Torpediniere e caccia giapponesi	30 cm (10)

Distanza di tiro utile		Dadi da tirare	
Tipo di nave	Raggio	Fiancata	Prua e poppa
Corazzate	Fino a 90 cm (36")	5	2
Incrociatori	Fino a 80 cm (32")	4	1
Incrociatori leggeri e ausiliari	Fino a 60 cm (23")	3	1
Torpediniere e caccia	Fino a 30 cm (12")	2	2

Tavola effetti cannoneggiamento	Raggio	
Risultato	45 cm (18")	46-90 cm (19"-36")
Non colpito	1-4	1-5
Colpito	5-6	6

Torpedo: Attacco e difesa tirano tre dadi, se l'attacco ottiene un sei e la difesa no il siluro va a segno. In caso di parità vine il difensore.

Effetti dei colpi	
Tipo di nave	Eliminato con
Corazzate	5
Incrociatore	3
Incrociatori leggeri e ausiliari	2
Torpediniere e caccia	2

Navi eliminate:
1 - 3 affondata (rimuovere dal tavolo)
4 - 6 Incendiata e abbandonata (lascia sul tavolo)

The great victory of the Japanese

 Japanese protected cruiser & Ironclad 1905 (2,7 Tons. 20 knots) 3rd, 4th, 5th sq.
Incrociatori protetti giapponesi e corazzata 1905 (2,7 ton. 20 nodi di velocità) 3a, 4a e 5a sq.

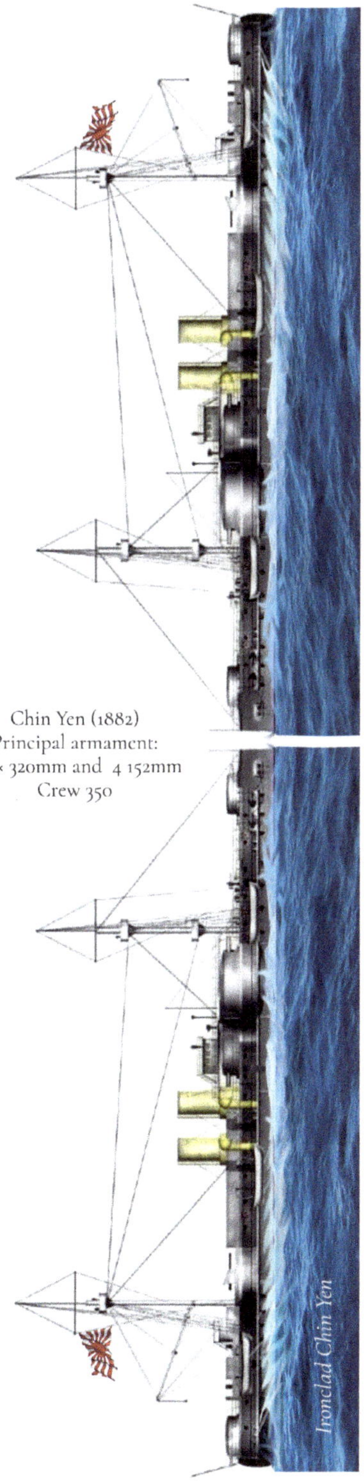

Chin Yen (1882)
Principal armament:
4 × 320mm and 4 152mm
Crew 350

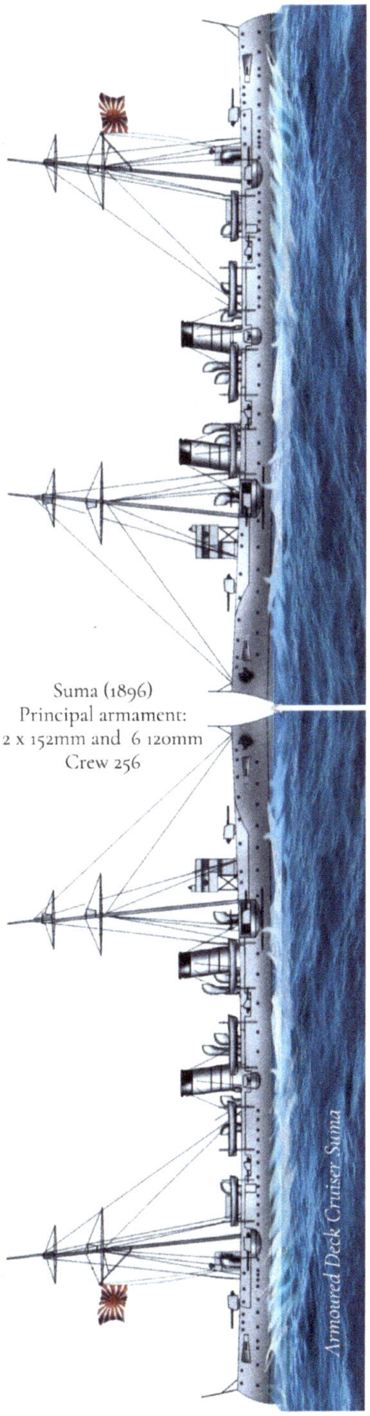

Suma (1896)
Principal armament:
2 x 152mm and 6 120mm
Crew 256

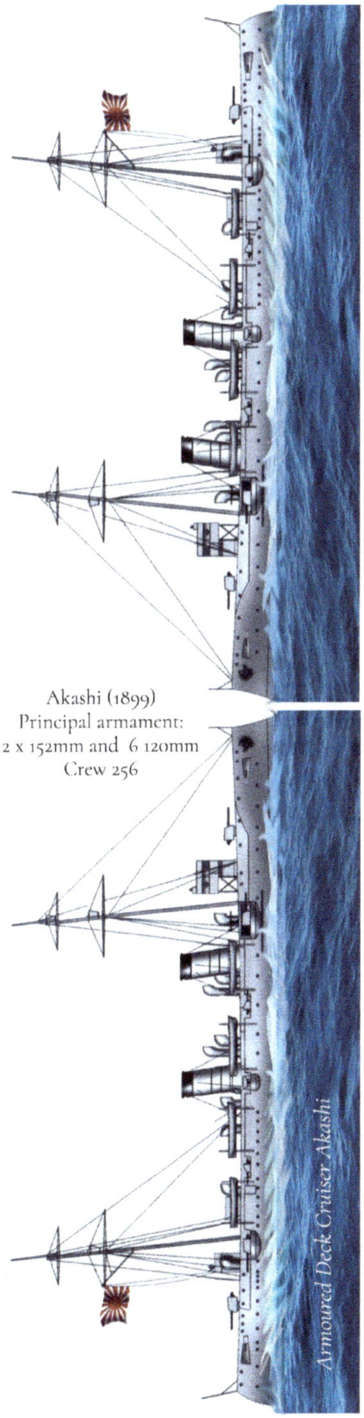

Akashi (1899)
Principal armament:
2 x 152mm and 6 120mm
Crew 256

Ironclad Chin Yen

Armoured Deck Cruiser Suma

Armoured Deck Cruiser Akashi

▲ At the end of the battle the Russians bury their fallen in the sea. Paint of Achille Beltrame.

Japanese protected cruiser & Aviso 1905 (3/1 Tons. 19/21 knots)
Incrociatori protetti giapponesi e Avvisi 1905 (3/1 ton. 9/21 nodi di velocità)

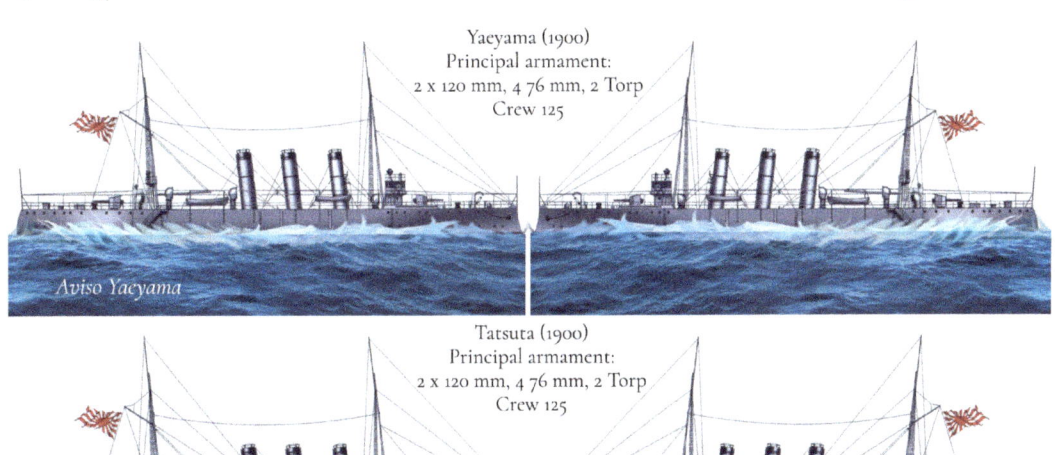

Yaeyama (1900)
Principal armament:
2 x 120 mm, 4 76 mm, 2 Torp
Crew 125

Aviso Yaeyama

Tatsuta (1900)
Principal armament:
2 x 120 mm, 4 76 mm, 2 Torp
Crew 125

Aviso Tatsuta

Chihaya (1900)
Principal armament:
2 x 120 mm, 4 76 mm, 2 Torp
Crew 125

Aviso Chihaya

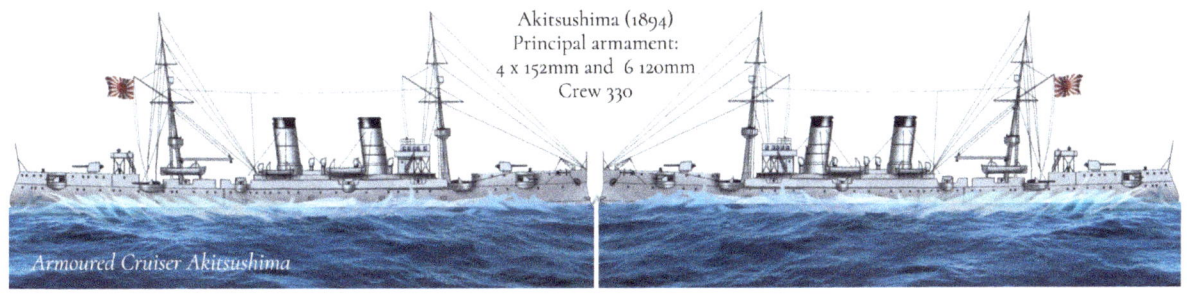

Akitsushima (1894)
Principal armament:
4 x 152mm and 6 120mm
Crew 330

Armoured Cruiser Akitsushima

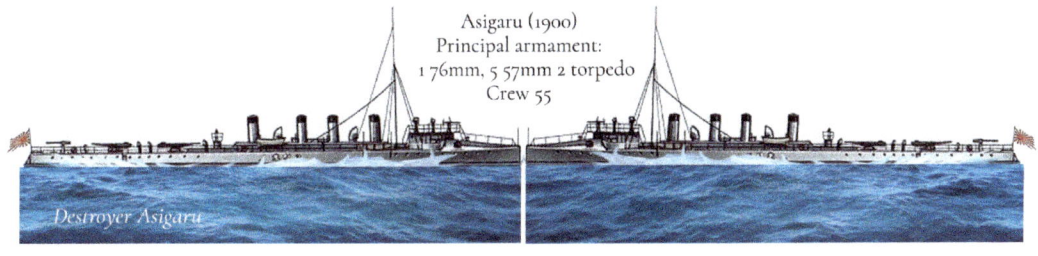

Asigaru (1900)
Principal armament:
1 76mm, 5 57mm 2 torpedo
Crew 55

Destroyer Asigaru

THE ARMY OF THE TWO FLEETS - ORDER OF BATTLE
LE FORMAZIONI DELLE DUE FLOTTE - ORDINE DI BATTAGLIA

RUSSIAN FLEET
(Second and Third Pacific Squadrons)

Battle Fleet at Tsushima

First Division *(Vice-Admiral Zinovy Rozhestvensky)*

-**Knyaz Suvorov** (Fleet Flagship) (*Borodino*-class battleship) Captain Vasily V. Ignatsius. (1902) 15 tons, 121 meter, crew 782 17,5 knot, armament: 4 305mm 12 152 mm 20 single 75.

-**Imperator Aleksandr III** (*Borodino*-class battleship) Captain Nikolai M. Bukhvostov. (1901) 15 tons, 121 meter, crew 782 18 knot armament: 4 305mm 12 152 mm 20 single 75.

-**Borodino** (*Borodino*-class battleship) Captain Petr. I. Serebrennikov. (1901) 14 tons, 121 meter, crew 782, knot 18 armament: 4 305mm 12 152 mm 20 single 75.

-**Oryol** (*Borodino*-class battleship) Captain Nikolai V. Jung. (1902) 14 tons, 121 m, Crew 855 knot 18. armament: 4 305mm 12 152 mm 20 single 75.

Second Division *(Captain Vladimir I. Bir)*

-**Oslyabya** (Flagship) (*Peresvet*-class battleship) Captain Vladimir I. Bir. (1898) 15 tons 132 meter, Crew

FLOTTA RUSSA
(seconda e terza squadra del Pacifico)

Flotta di battaglia a Tsushima

Prima Divisione *(Vice-a Zinovy Rozhestvensky)*

-**Knyaz Suvorov** (Ammiraglia) (*Borodino*-class Corazzata) Capitano Vasily V. Ignatsius. (1902) 15 ton., 121 metri, equipaggio 782 17,5 nodi, armamento: 4 305mm 12 152 mm 20 single 75.

-**Imperator Aleksandr III** (*Borodino*-class Corazzata) Capitano Nikolai M. Bukhvostov. (1901) 15 ton., 121 metri, equipaggio 782 18 nodi armamento: 4 305mm 12 152 mm 20 single 75.

-**Borodino** (*Borodino*-class Corazzata) Capitano Petr. I. Serebrennikov. (1901) 14 ton., 121 metri, equipaggio 782, nodi 18 armamento: 4 305mm 12 152 mm 20 single 75.

-**Oryol** (*Borodino*-class Corazzata) Capitano Nikolai V. Jung. (1902) 14 ton., 121 m, Equipaggio 855 nodi 18. armamento: 4 305mm 12 152 mm 20 single 75.

Second Divisione *(Capitano Vladimir I. Bir)*

-**Oslyabya** (Flagship) (*Peresvet*-class Corazzata) Capitano Vladimir I. Bir. (1898) 15 ton. 132 metri, Equi-

▲ The Russian battleship "Ironclad" Borodino.

 Japanese Destroyer 1905 (2/3 Tons. 30 knots 55/70 crew)
Cacciatorpedinieri giapponesi 1905 (2/3 ton. 30 nodi di velocità equipaggio 55/70)

Destroyer Akateuki

Fubuki (1900)
Principal armament:
1 76mm, 5 57mm 2 torpedo
Crew 55

Destroyer Fubuki

Destroyer Cazanami

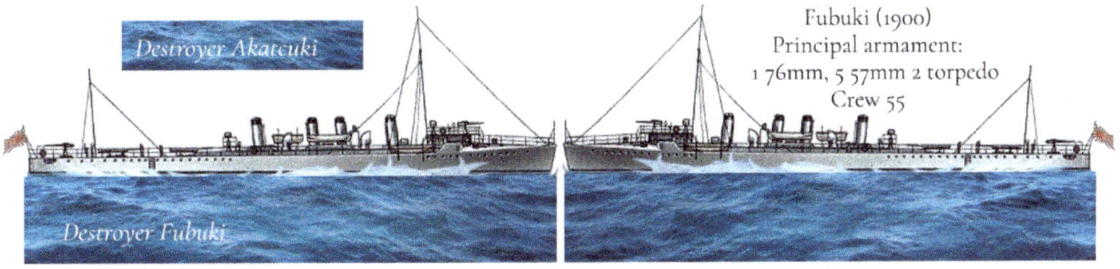

Oboro (1900)
Principal armament:
1 76mm, 5 57mm 2 torpedo
Crew 55

Destroyer Oboro

Destroyer Ugiri

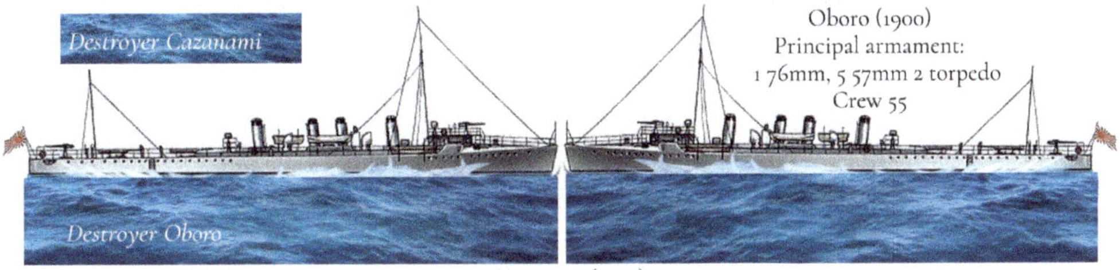

Usugumo (1900)
Principal armament:
1 76mm, 5 57mm 2 torpedo
Crew 55

Destroyer Kasumi

Destroyer Usugumo

Destroyer Murakumo

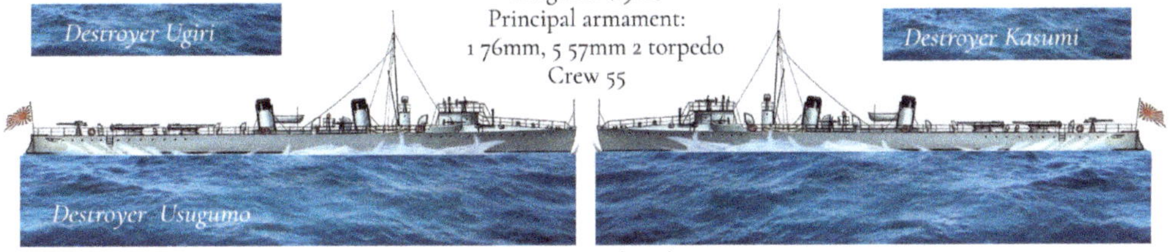

Sinomone (1900)
Principal armament:
1 76mm, 5 57mm 2 torpedo
Crew 55

Destroyer Sirakumi

Destroyer Sinomone

Destroyer Inadzuma

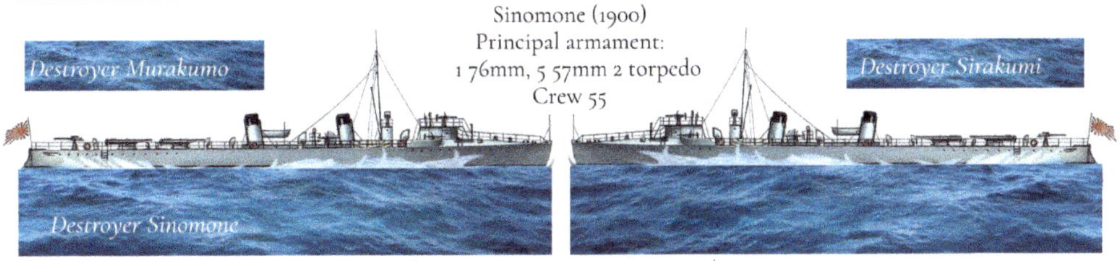

Arare (1900)
Principal armament:
1 76mm, 5 57mm 2 torpedo
Crew 55

Destroyer Sirakumo

Destroyer Arare

Destroyer Ariake

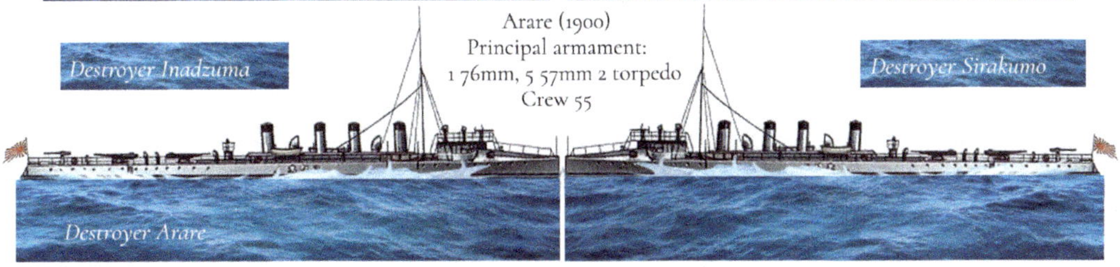

Harasume (1900)
Principal armament:
1 76mm, 5 57mm 2 torpedo
Crew 55

Destroyer Akebono

Destroyer Harasume

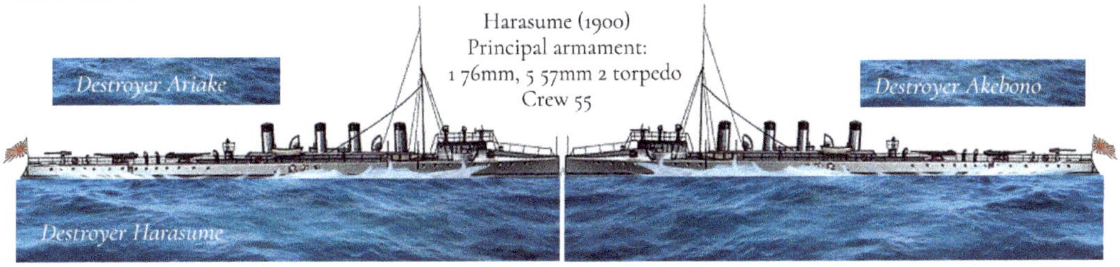

775, 18 knot armament: 4 254mm 11 152 mm 20 single 75.

-**Sissoi Veliky** (Battleship) Captain Mikhail V. Oserov. (1896) 10,5 tons, 107 meter, Crew 586, 16 knot armament 4 305mm, 6 152mm, 12 single 47mm.

-**Navarin** (Variant of *Trafalgar*-class battleship) Captain Baron B.A. Fitingof. (1896) 10 tons, 107 meter, Crew 440 15 knot armament: 4 305mm 8 152 mm 14 single 47.

-**Admiral Nakhimov** (Variant of *Imperieuse*-class armoured cruiser). (1885) 8 tons, 103 meter, Crew 650, 17 knot, armament 8 203mm, 10 152 mm, 4 110mm.

Third Division *(Rear-Admiral Nikolai Nebogatov)*

-**Imperator Nikolai I** (Flagship) (*Imperator Aleksandr II*-class battleship) Captain V. V. Smirnov. (1889) 10 tons, 105 meter, Crew 616, 14 knot, tons2 305mm, 6 152mm, 6 47mm.

-**General Admiral Graf Apraksin** (*Admiral Ushakov*-class coastal defence ship) Captain N. G. Liwin. (1899) 5 tons 81 meter, crew 406, 15 knot armament 3 254mm, 4 120mm, 10 x 47.

-**Admiral Seniavin** (*Admiral Ushakov*-class coastal defense ship) Captain S. J. Grogoryev. (1896) 5 tons 85 meter, crew 406, 16 knot armament 4 254mm, 4 120mm, 10 x 47.

-**Admiral Ushakov** (*Admiral Ushakov*-class coastal defense ship) Captain V.N. Miklukha-Maklai. (1895) 5 tons 87 meter, crew 404, 16 knot armament 4 254mm, 4 120mm, 6 x 47.

paggio 775, 18 nodi armamento: 4 254mm 11 152 mm 20 single 75.

-**Sissoi Veliky** (Corazzata) Capitano Mikhail V. Oserov. (1896) 10,5 ton., 107 metri, Equipaggio 586, 16 nodi armamento 4 305mm, 6 152mm, 12 single 47mm.

-**Navarin** (Variantee di *Trafalgar*-class Corazzata) Capitano Baron B.A. Fitingdi. (1896) 10 ton., 107 metri, Equipaggio 440 15 nodi armamento: 4 305mm 8 152 mm 14 single 47.

-**Ammiraglio Nakhimov** (Incrociatore corazzato). (1885) 8 ton., 103 metri, Equipaggio 650, 17 nodi, armamento 8 203mm, 10 152 mm, 4 110mm.

Terza Divisione *(Vice-Ammiraglio Nikolai Nebogatov)*

-**Imperator Nikolai I** (Flagship) (*Imperator Aleksandr II*-class Corazzata) Capitano V. V. Smirnov. (1889) 10 ton., 105 metri, Equipaggio 616, 14 nodi, ton.2 305mm, 6 152mm, 6 47mm.

-**General Ammiraglio Graf Apraksin** (*Ammiraglio Ushakov*-class Corazzata vecchio tipo) Capitano N. G. Liwin. (1899) 5 ton. 81 metri, equipaggio 406, 15 nodi armamento 3 254mm, 4 120mm, 10 x 47.

-**Ammiraglio Seniavin** (*Ammiraglio Ushakov*-class Nave difesa costale) Capitano S. J. Grogoryev. (1896) 5 ton. 85 metri, equipaggio 406, 16 nodi armamento 4 254mm, 4 120mm, 10 x 47.

-**Ammiraglio Ushakov** (*Ammiraglio Ushakov*-class Nave difesa costale) Capitano V.N. Miklukha-Maklai. (1895) 5 ton. 87 metri, equipaggio 404, 16 nodi armamento 4 254mm, 4 120mm, 6 x 47.

▲ Russian Ironclad: Osliabya, Peresveth and Pobieda.

 Japanese Torpedo 1905 1,5 ton, 45m. 29 Kn crew 30. Arm. 1 57mm 2 42mm e 3 torpedo
Torpedo giapponesi 1905 1,5 ton, 45m. 29 nod Eq. 30. Arm. 1 57mm 2 42mm e 3 torpedo

Torpedo Nr. 70
Torpedo Nr. 68
Torpedo nr. 69
Torpedo Nr. 67
Torpedo Kidgi
Torpedo Kari
Torpedo Manadzuru
Torpedo Chidori
Torpedo Hayabusa
Torpedo Odori
Torpedo Haro
Torpedo Tsubame
Torpedo Kasasagi
Torpedo Aotaka

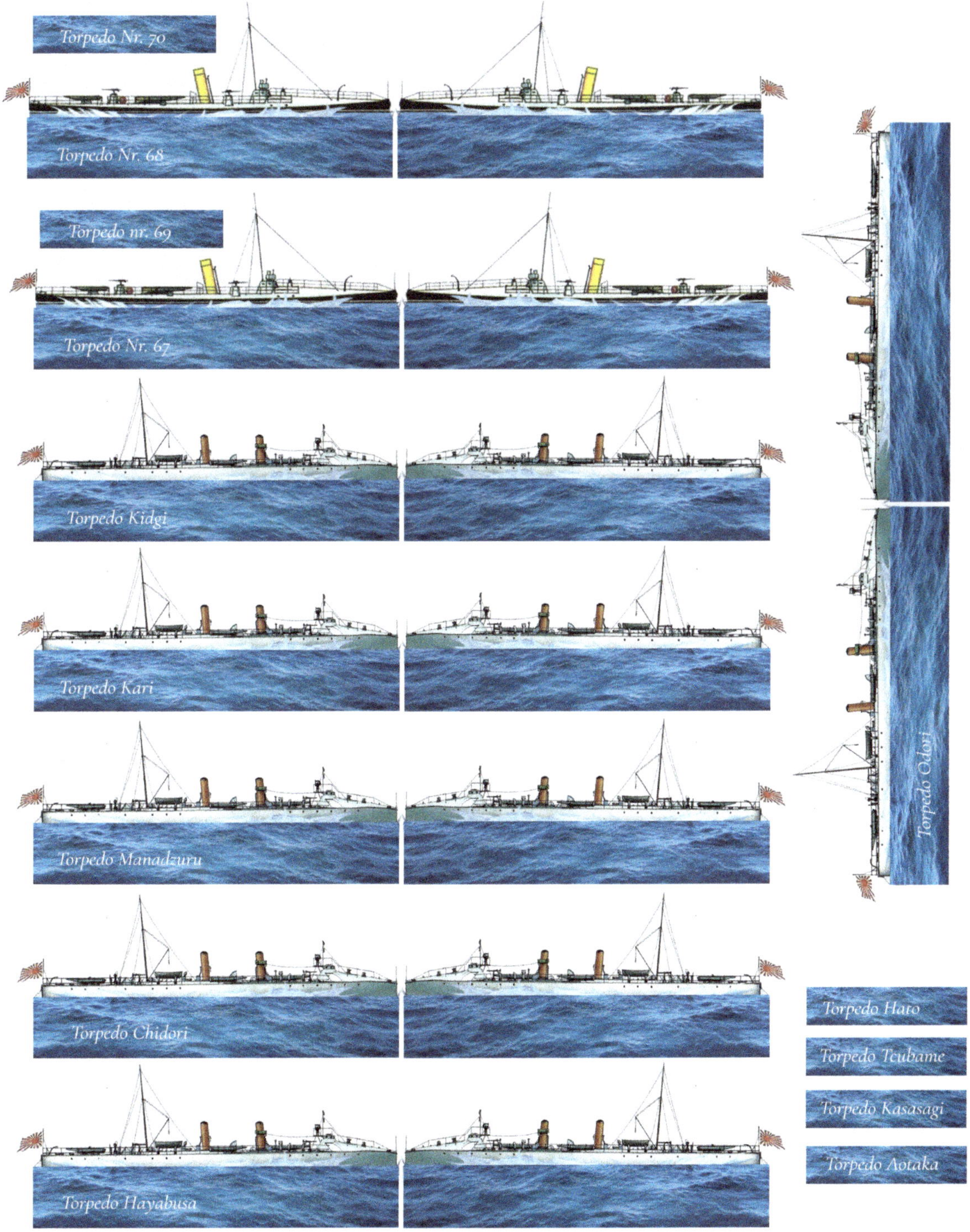

Attached Cruisers
Zhemchug (*Izumrud*-class protected cruiser). (1904) 3 tons 110 meter, 354 crew, 23 knot armament 8 120mm. 4 47mm.
Izumrud (*Izumrud*-class protected cruiser). (1904) 3 tons 110 meter, 350 crew, 24 knot armament 8 120mm. 4 47mm.

First Cruiser Division (*Rear-Admiral Oskar Enkvist*)
Oleg (Flagship) (*Bogatyr*-class protected cruiser). (1904) 7 tons 134 meter, 576 crew, 23 knot armament 12 150mm. 8 47mm.
Aurora (*Pallada*-class protected cruiser). (1896) 7 tons 127 meter, 590 crew, 19 knot armament 8 152mm 24 75mm 8 37mm.
Dmitrii Donskoi (Armoured cruiser). (1885) 6 tons 94 meter, 591 crew, 17 knot armament 2 203mm 5 152 mm.
Vladimir Monomakh (Armoured cruiser). (1883) 6 tons 91 meter, 591 crew, 15 knot armament 4 203mm 6 152mm.

Second Scouting Division
Svetlana (Protected cruiser). (1897) 3,9 tons 101 meter, 401 crew, 21 knot armament 6 152mm 10 47mm.
Ural (Armed merchant cruiser) (1890) 7,8 tons 141 meter, 510 crew, 20 knot armament 1 305 mm 2 x 120mm e 4 76mm.

Incrociatori aggiunti
Zhemchug (*Izumrud*-class Incrociatore protetto). (1904) 3 ton. 110 metri, 354 equipaggio, 23 nodi armamento 8 120mm. 4 47mm.
Izumrud (*Izumrud*-class Incrociatore protetto). (1904) 3 ton. 110 metri, 350 equipaggio, 24 nodi armamento 8 120mm. 4 47mm.

Prima Divisione incrociatori (*Vice-Ammiraglio O. Enkvist*)
Oleg (Flagship) (*Bogatyr*-class Incrociatore protetto). (1904) 7 ton. 134 metri, 576 equipaggio, 23 nodi armamento 12 150mm. 8 47mm.
Aurora (*Pallada*-class Incrociatore protetto). (1896) 7 ton. 127 metri, 590 equipaggio, 19 nodi armamento 8 152mm 24 75mm 8 37mm.
Dmitrii Donskoi (Incrociatore corazzato). (1885) 6 ton. 94 metri, 591 equipaggio, 17 nodi armamento 2 203mm 5 152 mm.
Vladimir Monomakh (Incrociatore corazzato). (1883) 6 ton. 91 metri, 591 equipaggio, 15 nodi armamento 4 203mm 6 152mm.

Seconda Divisione esplorante
Svetlana (Incrociatore protetto). (1897) 3,9 ton. 101 metri, 401 equipaggio, 21 nodi arma. 6 152mm 10 47mm.
Ural (Incrociatore adattato) (1890) 7,8 ton. 141 metri, 510 equipaggio, 20 nodi armamento 1 305 mm 2 x 120mm e 4 76mm.

▲ The Russian battleship "Ironclad" Poltava.

1904-1905 RUSSO-JAPAN WAR - JAPANESE ARMY - 1904-1905 GUERRA RUSSO GIAPPONESE - ESERCITO GIAPPONESE

Destroyer Flotilla
First Destroyer Division
Byedovy
Buiny
Bravy leith. P.P. Durnovo
Buistry
Second Destroyer Division
Blestyashchy cap. S. A. Shamov
Bezuprechny leith. O.O. Richter
Bodry cap. I.A.Matusevich 2nd
Gromky cap. . G.F. Kern
Grozny cap. K.K. Andrzhievsky

(1900-1904) 3,5 ton, 64 meter, 26 knot, crew 60 di media   armament 1 75mm 5 47mm 2 torpedo

Transport Squadron
Auxiliaries
Almaz (Armed Yacht classified as 2nd class cruiser). 3,3 tons, 111,5 meter, Crew 336, 19 knots. Armament: 4x 75mm, 8 x 47mm.
Anadyr (Transport/Merchant Ship). 7 tons, 151 meter, 10 knots. cap. V.F. Ponomarev
Irtuish (Transport/Merchant Ship). cap. K.L. Ergomyshev
Kamchatka (Repair Ship). cap. A.I.Stepanov
Koreya (Ammunition Ship) Doc. Med. I.O.Zubov
Rus (Fleet Tug) cap. 1 bit V.Pernitz
Svir (Fleet Tug) warrant officer G.A. Rosenfeld
Oryol (Hospital Ship) Cap. Ya.K. Lokhmatov
Kostroma (Hospital Ship) Colonel N. Smelsky

Flottiglia di cacciatorpedinieri
Prima Divisione Caccia
Byedovy
Buiny
Bravy Ten. P.P. Durnovo
Buistry
Seconda Divisione Caccia
Blestyashchy cap. S. A. Shamov
Bezuprechny Ten.. O.O. Richter
Bodry cap. I.A.Matusevich 2nd
Gromky cap. . G.F. Kern
Grozny cap. K.K. Andrzhievsky

(1900-1904) 3,5 ton, 64 metri, 26 nodi, equipaggio 60 di media   armamento 1 75mm 5 47mm 2 torpedo

Squadrone Trasporti
Navi ausiliarie
Almaz (Yacht riconvertito in incrociatore). 3,3 ton., 111,5 metri, Equipaggio 336, 19 nodi. Armamento: 4x 75mm, 8 x 47mm.
Anadyr (Trasporto/mercantileShip). 7 ton., 151 metri, 10 nodi. cap. V.F. Ponomarev
Irtuish (Trasporto/mercantileShip). cap. K.L. Ergomyshev
Kamchatka (Nave officina). cap. A.I.Stepanov
Koreya (nave munizioni) Doc. Med. I.O.Zubov
Rus (Rimorchiatore) cap. 1 bit V.Pernitz
Svir (Rimorchiatore) Ten. G.A. Rosenfeld
Oryol (Nave ospedale) Cap. Ya.K. Lokhmatov
Kostroma (Nave ospedale) Colonello N. Smelsky

▲ The Russian battleship "Ironclad" Zar Alexander III

Russian Squadron Ironclad 1905 (15 Tons. 18 knots) 1st Div.
Corazzate russe 1905 (15 ton. 18 nodi di velocità) 1a div.

Alexander III (1901)
Principal armament:
4 305mm 12
152 mm 20 single 75
Crew 782

Orel (1902)
Principal armament:
4 305mm 12
152 mm 20 single 75
Crew 855

Borodino (1901)
Principal armament:
4 305mm 12
152 mm 20 single 75
Crew 782

JAPANESE COMBINED FLEET
First Squadron
First Division *(Admiral Heihachirō Tōgō)*

Mikasa (Flagship) (variant of *Majestic*-class battleship) Captain Hihajiro Ijichi. (1900) 15,4 tons 132 meter 18 knot crew 836 armament: 2 × twin 30.5 14 single 15,2 cm 20 single 76mm.
Shikishima (*Shikishima*-class battleship) Captain Izo Teregaki. (1898) 15 tons 133 meter 18 knot crew 741 armament: 2 × twin 30.5 14 single 15,2 cm 20 single 76mm.
Fuji (*Fuji*-class battleship) Captain Kazu Matsomoto (1896) 12,5 tons 125 meter 18 knot crew 650 armament: 2 × twin 30.5 10 single 15,2 cm 20 single 76mm.
Asahi (Variant of *Shikishima* class) Captain Hikohachi Yamada. (1900) 15,2 tons 129 meter 18 knot crew 773 armament: 2 × twin 30.5 14 single 15,2 cm 20 single 76mm.
Kasuga (*Kasuga*-class armoured cruiser). (1903) 7,7 ton 112 meter 20 knot crew 600 armament: 1 × twin 25,4 1 × twin 20,3 14 single 15,2 cm 12 single 76mm.
Nisshin (*Kasuga*-class armoured cruiser). (1903) 7,7 ton 112 meter 20 knot crew 560 armament: 2 × twin 20,3 .5 14 single 15,2 cm 12 single 76mm
Tatsuta (Dispatch Vessel) (1901) 1,2 tons 70-83 meter, 21 knot, 100-125 crew. Armament: 2 x120 e 4 x 76 e 2 torpedo.

FLOTTA GIAPPONESE
Prima Squadra
Prima Divisione *(Ammiraglio Heihachirō Tōgō)*

Mikasa (Ammiraglia) (variante di *Majestic*-class Corazzata) Capitano Hihajiro Ijichi. (1900) 15,4 ton. 132 metri 18 nodi equipaggio 836 armamento: 2 × twin 30.5 14 single 15,2 cm 20 single 76mm.
Shikishima (*Shikishima*-class Corazzata) Capitano Izo Teregaki. (1898) 15 ton. 133 metri 18 nodi equipaggio 741 armamento: 2 × twin 30.5 14 single 15,2 cm 20 single 76mm.
Fuji (*Fuji*-class Corazzata) Capitano Kazu Matsomoto (1896) 12,5 ton. 125 metri 18 nodi equipaggio 650 armamento: 2 × twin 30.5 10 single 15,2 cm 20 single 76mm.
Asahi (Variante di *Shikishima* class) Capitano Hikohachi Yamada. (1900) 15,2 ton. 129 metri 18 nodi equipaggio 773 armamento: 2 × twin 30.5 14 single 15,2 cm 20 single 76mm.
Kasuga (*Kasuga*-class Incrociatore corazzato). (1903) 7,7 ton 112 metri 20 nodi equipaggio 600 armamento: 1 × twin 25,4 1 × twin 20,3 14 single 15,2 cm 12 single 76mm.
Nisshin (*Kasuga*-class Incrociatore corazzato). (1903) 7,7 ton 112 metri 20 nodi equipaggio 560 armamento: 2 × twin 20,3 .5 14 single 15,2 cm 12 single 76mm
Tatsuta (Avviso) (1901) 1,2 ton. 70-83 metri, 21 nodi, 100-125 equipaggio. Armamento: 2 x120 e 4 x 76 e 2 torpedo.

▲ The Japanese Imperial Fleet at sea on manoeuvres, 1902-04 by William Lionel Wylie

Russian Squadron Ironclad 1905 (15 Tons.18 knots) 1st & 2nd Div.
Corazzate russe 1905 (15 ton. 18 nodi di velocità) 1a e 2a div.

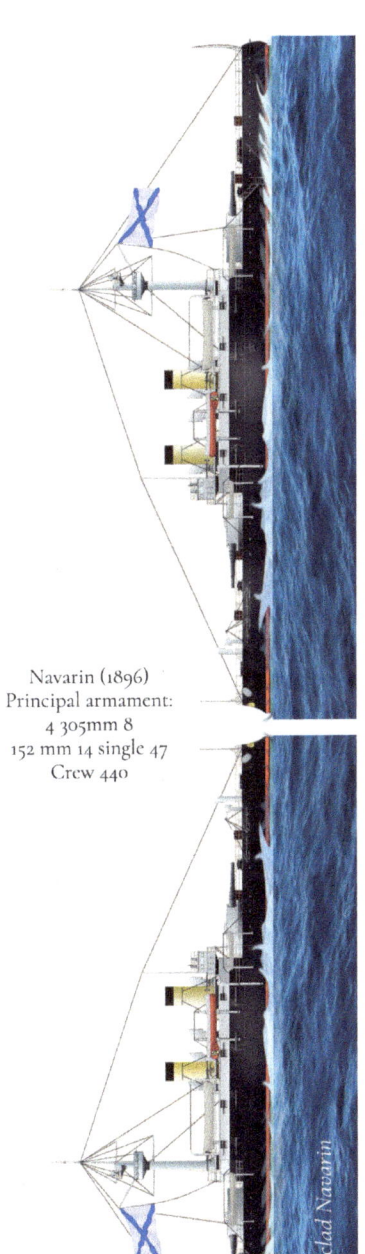

Navarin (1896)
Principal armament:
4 305mm 8
152 mm 14 single 47
Crew 440

Squadron Ironclad Navarin

Oslyabya (1898)
Principal armament:
4 254mm 11
152 mm 20 single 75
Crew 775

Squadron Ironclad Oysabya

Suvorov (1902)
Principal armament:
4 305mm 12
152 mm 20 single 75
Crew 782

Squadron Ironclad Fleet Flagship Suvorov

First Destroyer Division
: *Harusame* (*Harusame*-class destroyer)
  Fubuki (*Harusame*-class destroyer)
  Ariake (*Harusame*-class destroyer)
  Akatsuki (Ex-Russian destroyer *Reshitel'nyi*)
  1900 3 tons, 67 meter 30 knot, crew 55 armament 1 76mm, 5 57mm e 2 torpedo

Second Destroyer Division
: *Oboro* (*Ikazuchi*-class destroyer)
  Inazuma (*Ikazuchi*-class destroyer)
  Ikazuchi (*Ikazuchi*-class destroyer)
  Akebono (*Ikazuchi*-class destroyer)

  1900 3 tons, 67 meter 30 knot, crew 55 armament 1 76mm, 5 57mm e 2 torpedo

Ninth Torpedo-Boat Division
: *Aotaka* (*Hayabusa*-class torpedo boat)
  Kari (*Hayabusa*-class torpedo boat)
  Tsubame (*Hayabusa*-class torpedo boat)
  Hato (*Hayabusa*-class torpedo boat)

Third Division (*Vice-Admiral Shigetō Dewa*)
: *Kasagi* (*Kasagi*-class protected cruiser) Captain Tanin Yamaya. (1898) 4,9 tons 114 meter 22 knot crew 405 armament: 2 × 20,3 10 single 12,0 12 single 76mm.
  Chitose (*Kasagi*-class protected cruiser). (1899) 4,9 tons 115 meter 22 knot crew 405 armament: 2 × 20,3 10 single 12,0 12 single 76mm.

Prima Divisione Cacciatorpediniere
: *Harusame* (*Harusame*-class Caccia)
  Fubuki (*Harusame*-class Caccia)
  Ariake (*Harusame*-class Caccia)
  Akatsuki (Ex-Russian Caccia *Reshitel'nyi*)
  1900 3 ton., 67 metri 30 nodi, equipaggio 55 armamento 1 76mm, 5 57mm e 2 torpedo

Seconda Divisione Cacciatorpediniere
: *Oboro* (*Ikazuchi*-class Caccia)
  Inazuma (*Ikazuchi*-class Caccia)
  Ikazuchi (*Ikazuchi*-class Caccia)
  Akebono (*Ikazuchi*-class Caccia)

  1900 3 ton., 67 metri 30 nodi, equipaggio 55 armamento 1 76mm, 5 57mm e 2 torpedo

Nona Divisione Torpedo
: *Aotaka* (*Hayabusa*-class Torpediniere)
  Kari (*Hayabusa*-class Torpediniere)
  Tsubame (*Hayabusa*-class Torpediniere)
  Hato (*Hayabusa*-class Torpediniere)

Terza Divisione (*Vice-Ammiraglio Shigetō Dewa*)
: *Kasagi* (*Kasagi*-class Incrociatore protetto) Capitano Tanin Yamaya. (1898) 4,9 ton. 114 metri 22 nodi equipaggio 405 armamento: 2 × 20,3 10 single 12,0 12 single 76mm.
  Chitose (*Kasagi*-class Incrociatore protetto). (1899) 4,9 ton. 115 metri 22 nodi equipaggio 405 armamento: 2 × 20,3 10 single 12,0 12 single 76mm.

▲ Japanese battleships in action, the Shikishima, Fuji, Asahi and Mikasa. Courteously by Wikipedia

 Russian Squadron Ironclad 1905 (10/8 Tons. 16 knots) 2nd & 33dDiv.
Corazzate russe 1905 (10/8 ton. 16 nodi di velocità) a e 3a div.

Imperator Nikolai I (1889)
Principal armament:
2 305mm 6
152 mm 6 single 47
Crew 616

Squadron Ironclad Imperator Nikola I

Sisoy Veliki (1896)
Principal armament:
4 305 mm 12
152 mm 12 single 47
Crew 586

Squadron Ironclad Sisoy Veliki

Admiral Nakhimov (1885)
Principal armament:
8 203 mm 10
152 mm 6 single 47
Crew 650

Armoured cruiser Admiral Nakhimov

Niitaka (*Niitaka*-class protected cruiser). 1° sq (1902) 3,4 tons 102 meter 20 knot crew 290 armament: 6 single 152 e 10 76

Otowa (variant of *Niitaka*-class protected cruiser) 1° sq. (1904) 3,0 tons 98 meter 21 knot crew 290 armament: 2 single 152 e 6 120 .

Fourth Destroyer Division
Asagiri (*Harusame*-class destroyer)
Murasame (*Harusame*-class destroyer)
Shirakumo (*Shirakumo*-class destroyer)
Asashio (*Shirakumo*-class destroyer)
1900 3 tons, 67 meter 30 knot, crew 55 armament 1 76mm, 5 57mm e 2 torpedo *Each carrying 8 x 100 lb Mines*

Second Squadron
Second Division (*Vice-Admiral Hikonojō Kamimura*)
Izumo (Flagship) (*Izumo*-class armoured cruiser). (1898) 9,5 tons 134 meter 21 knot crew 672 armament: 2 × twin 20,3 .5 14 single 15,2 cm 12 single 76mm.
Azuma (Armoured cruiser) Rokuro Yashiro. (1899) 9,7 tons 137 meter 21 knot crew 670 armament: 2 × twin 20,3 .5 12 single 15,2 cm 12 single 76mm.
Tokiwa (*Asama*-class armoured cruiser) Captain Reijiro Kawashima. (1898) 9,7 tons 134 meter 21 knot crew 676 armament: 2 × twin 20,3 .5 14 single 15,2 cm 12 single 76m.

Niitaka (*Niitaka*-class Incrociatore protetto). 1° sq (1902) 3,4 ton. 102 metri 20 nodi equipaggio 290 armamento: 6 single 152 e 10 76

Otowa (variante di *Niitaka*-class Incrociatore protetto) 1° sq. (1904) 3,0 ton. 98 metri 21 nodi equipaggio 290 armamento: 2 single 152 e 6 120 .

Quarta Divisione Cacciatorpediniere
Asagiri (*Harusame*-class Caccia)
Murasame (*Harusame*-class Caccia)
Shirakumo (*Shirakumo*-class Caccia)
Asashio (*Shirakumo*-class Caccia)
1900 3 ton., 67 metri 30 nodi, equipaggio 55 armamento 1 76mm, 5 57mm e 2 torpedo *più ton. di min.*

Seconda Squadra
Seconda Divisione (*Vice-Ammiraglio Hikonojō Kamimura*)
Izumo (Ammiraglia) (*Izumo*-class Incrociatore corazzato). (1898) 9,5 ton. 134 metri 21 nodi equipaggio 672 armamento: 2 × twin 20,3 .5 14 single 15,2 cm 12 single 76mm.
Azuma (Incrociatore corazzato) Rokuro Yashiro. (1899) 9,7 ton. 137 metri 21 nodi equipaggio 670 arm.: 2 × twin 20,3 .5 12 single 15,2 cm 12 single 76mm.
Tokiwa (*Asama*-class Incrociatore corazzato) Capitano Reijiro Kawashima. (1898) 9,7 ton. 134 metri 21 nodi equipaggio 676 armamento: 2 × twin 20,3 .5 14 single 15,2 cm 12 single 76m.

▲ The Japanese Imperial Ship Asama.

Russian Squadron Ironclad 1905 (5 Tons. 16 knots) 3rd. Div.
Corazzate russe 1905 (5 ton. 16 nodi di velocità) 3a div.

Imperator Ad. Ushakov (1895)
Principal armament:
4 254mm
4 120 mm 6 single 47
Crew 404

Ad. Senyavin (1896)
Principal armament:
4 254mm
4 120 mm 10 single 47
Crew 406

Admiral Apraksin (1899)
Principal armament:
3 254mm
4 120 mm 10 single 47
Crew 406

Squadron Ironclad Admiral Ushakov

Squadron Ironclad Admiral Senyavin

Armoured cruiser Admiral Apraksin

Yakumo (Armoured cruiser). (1901) 9,5 tons 132 meter 20 knot crew 672 armament: 2 × twin 20,3 .5 12 single 15,2 cm 12 single 76mm

Asama (*Asama*-class armoured cruiser) (1899) 9,7 tons 134 meter 21 knot crew 676 armament: 2 × twin 20,3 .5 14 single 15,2 cm 12 single 76mm.

Iwate (*Izumo*-class armoured cruiser). (1901) 9,5 tons 134 meter 21 knot crew 672 armament: 2 × twin 20,3 .5 14 single 15,2 cm 12 single 76mm.

Chihaya (Dispatch Vessel). (1901) 1,2 tons 70-83 meter, 21 knot, 100-125 crew. Armament: 2 x120 e 4 x 76 e 2 torpedo.

Fifth Destroyer Division

Shiranui (*Murakumo*-class destroyer)
Murakumo (*Murakumo*-class destroyer)
Yugiri (*Murakumo*-class destroyer)
Kagero (*Murakumo*-class destroyer)
1900 3 tons, 67 meter 30 knot, crew 55 armament 1 76mm, 5 57mm e 2 torpedo.

Third Destroyer Division

Shinonome (*Murakumo*-class destroyer)
Usugumo (*Murakumo*-class destroyer)
Kasumi (*Akatsuki*-class destroyer)
Sazanami (*Ikazuchi*-class destroyer)
1900 3 tons, 67 meter 30 knot, crew 55 armament 1 76mm, 5 57mm e 2 torpedo

Yakumo (Incrociatore corazzato). (1901) 9,5 ton. 132 metri 20 nodi equipaggio 672 armamento: 2 × twin 20,3 .5 12 single 15,2 cm 12 single 76mm

Asama (*Asama*-class Incrociatore corazzato) (1899) 9,7 ton. 134 metri 21 nodi equipaggio 676 armamento: 2 × twin 20,3 .5 14 single 15,2 cm 12 single 76mm.

Iwate (*Izumo*-class Incrociatore corazzato). (1901) 9,5 ton. 134 metri 21 nodi equipaggio 672 armamento: 2 × twin 20,3 .5 14 single 15,2 cm 12 single 76mm.

Chihaya (Dispatch Vessel). (1901) 1,2 ton. 70-83 metri, 21 nodi, 100-125 equipaggio. Armamento: 2 x120 e 4 x 76 e 2 torpedo.

Quinta Divisione Cacciatorpediniere

Shiranui (*Murakumo*-class Caccia)
Murakumo (*Murakumo*-class Caccia)
Yugiri (*Murakumo*-class Caccia)
Kagero (*Murakumo*-class Caccia)
1900 3 ton., 67 metri 30 nodi, equipaggio 55 armamento 1 76mm, 5 57mm e 2 torpedo

Terza Divisione Cacciatorpediniere

Shinonome (*Murakumo*-class Caccia)
Usugumo (*Murakumo*-class Caccia)
Kasumi (*Akatsuki*-class Caccia)
Sazanami (*Ikazuchi*-class Caccia)
1900 3 ton., 67 metri 30 nodi, equipaggio 55 armamento 1 76mm, 5 57mm e 2 torpedo

▲ The Japanese Imperial Ship Azuma.

 Russian Cruiser 1905 (7/3 Tons. 23 knots) 1st Div. & added
Incrociatori russi 1905 (7/3 ton. 23 nodi di velocità) 1a div. e aggiunti

Oleg (1904)
Principal armament:
12 150mm
8 single 47
Crew 576

Aurora (1896)
Principal armament:
8 152 mm
24 75mm 8 single 37
Crew 590

Zhemchug (1904)
Principal armament:
8 120mm
4 47mm
Crew 354

Fourth Division (*Rear-Admiral Sotokichi Uryu*)

Naniwa (*Naniwa*-class protected cruiser) (1885) 3,7 ton 92 meter 19 knot crew 325 armament: 2 single 260 e 6 152.

Takachiho (*Naniwa*-class protected cruiser). (1885) 3,7 ton 92 meter 19 knot crew 325 armament: 2 single 260 e 6 152.

Akashi (*Suma*-class protected cruiser) (1899) 2,7 tons 94 meter 20 knot crew 256 armament: 2 152mm 6 120mm.

Tsushima (*Niitaka*-class protected cruiser). (1902) 3,4 tons 102 meter 20 knot crew 290 armament: 6 single 152 e 10 76.

Third Squadron

Fifth Division (*Vice-Admiral Shichirō Kataoka*)

Itsukushima (Flagship) (*Matsushima*-class protected cruiser). (1891) 4,3 tons 92 meter 17 knot crew 360 armament: 1 320mm 11 47mm.

Chin'en (Rebuilt ex-Chinese turret ship *Zhenyuan*). (1882) 7,5 tons 94 meter 15 knot crew 350 armament: 4 305mm, 4 152mm.

Matsushima (*Matsushima*-class protected cruiser). (1892) 4,3 tons 92 meter 17 knot crew 360 armament: 1 320mm 12 47mm.

Hashidate (*Matsushima*-class protected cruiser). (1894) 4,3 tons 92 meter 17 knot crew 360 armament: 1 320mm 11 47mm.

Yaeyama (Dispatch Vessel). (1901) 1,2 tons 70-83 meter, 21 knot, 100-125 crew. Armament: 2 x120 e 4 x 76 e 2 torpedo.

▲ The Japanese Imperial FlagShip Mikasa.

 Russian Cruiser 1905 (6/3 Tons. 23 knots) 1st Div. & added
Incrociatori russi 1905 (6/3 ton. 23 nodi di velocità) 1a div. e aggiunti

Donskoi (1885)
Principal armament:
  2 203mm
  5 152mm
  Crew 591

1st rank cruiser Donskoi

Monomahk (1883)
Principal armament:
  4 203mm
  6 152mm
  Crew 591

1st rank cruiser Monomahk

Izumrud (1904)
Principal armament:
  8 120mm
  4 47mm
  Crew 350

2nd rank cruiser Izumrud

Eleventh Torpedo-Boat Division
No. 73
No. 72
No. 74
No. 75
1900-1904 1,5 tons, 45meter 29 knot crew 30 , armament 1 57mm 2 42mm e 3 torpedo

Sixth Division *(Rear-Admiral Togo Masaji)*
Suma (*Suma*-class protected cruiser). (1896) 2,7 tons 94 meter 20 knot crew 256 armament: 2 152mm 6 120mm.
Chiyoda (protected cruiser). (1890) 2,5 tons 95 meter 19 knot crew 350 armament: 10 single 12,0 .
Akitsushima (2nd class protected cruiser). 1894, 3 tons, 92 meter, 19 knot, crew 330, armament 4 152mm, 6 120mm 4 47mm.
Izumi (2nd class protected cruiser). (1894) 3, ton 82 meter 19 knot crew 296 armament: 2 152 6 120 .

Tenth Torpedo-Boat Division
No. 43
No. 42
No. 40
No. 41
1900-1904 1,5 tons, 45meter 29 knot crew 30 , armament 1 57mm 2 42mm e 3 torpedo

Fifteenth Torpedo Boat Division
Hibari (*Hayabusa*-class torpedo boat)
Sagi (*Hayabusa*-class torpedo boat)
Hashitaki (*Hayabusa*-class torpedo boat)
Uzura (*Hayabusa*-class torpedo boat)
1900-1904 1,5 tons, 45meter 29 knot crew 30 , armament 1 57mm 2 42mm e 3 torpedo

Undicesima Divisione Torpedo
No. 73
No. 72
No. 74
No. 75
1900-1904 1,5 ton., 45metri 29 nodi equipaggio 30 , armamento 1 57mm 2 42mm e 3 torpedo

Sesta Divisione *(Vice-Ammiraglio Togo Masaji)*
Suma (*Suma*-class Incrociatore protetto). (1896) 2,7 ton. 94 metri 20 nodi equipaggio 256 armamento: 2 152mm 6 120mm.
Chiyoda (Incrociatore protetto). (1890) 2,5 ton. 95 metri 19 nodi equipaggio 350 armamento: 10 single 12,0
Akitsushima (2nd class Incrociatore protetto). 1894, 3 ton., 92 metri, 19 nodi, equipaggio 330, armamento 4 152mm, 6 120mm 4 47mm.
Izumi (2nd class Incrociatore protetto). (1894) 3, ton 82 metri 19 nodi equipaggio 296 armamento: 2 152 6 120 .

Decima Divisione Torpedo
No. 43
No. 42
No. 40
No. 41
1900-1904 1,5 ton., 45metri 29 nodi equipaggio 30 , armamento 1 57mm 2 42mm e 3 torpedo

Quindicesima Divisione Torpedo
Hibari (*Hayabusa*-class Torpediniere)
Sagi (*Hayabusa*-class Torpediniere)
Hashitaki (*Hayabusa*-class Torpediniere)
Uzura (*Hayabusa*-class Torpediniere)
1900-1904 1,5 ton., 45metri 29 nodi equipaggio 30 , armamento 1 57mm 2 42mm e 3 torpedo

▲ Russian warship sustains heavy damage during the battle of Tsushima May 27–28, 1905

Russian Auxiliaries cruiser 1905 (3,5/7 Tons.19-21 knots)
Incrociatori ausuliari russi 1905 (3,5/7 ton. 19-21 nodi di velocità)

Svetlana(1897)
Principal armament:
 6 152mm
 10 47mm
 21 knot
 Crew 401

Armoured Deck Cruiser Svetlana

Almaz (1903)
Principal armament:
 3 120mm
 10 75mm
 19 knot
 Crew 336

Armed Yacht Cruiser Almaz

Ural(1890)
Principal armament:
 1 305mm
 3 120mm & 4 76mm
 20 knot
 Crew 510

Armed Merchant cruiser Ural

27-28 MAY 1905 THE BATTLE
27-28 MAGGIO 1905 LA BATTAGLIA

The Russian Pacific fleet, after an incredible voyage that took it from St. Petersburg to the Far East, tries to force the Tsushima Canal, an island between Japan and Korea, a compulsory route to Vladivostok, the last Russian fortress after the fall of Port Arthur. The Russian ships, beyond the technological inferiority, are in very bad conditions for the long journey and with tired and demoralised crews. On the other hand, the Japanese have had plenty of time to prepare themselves for this clash that is taking place at home with the good prospect of being able to break through.

Forces in the field

The Russian team is composed of the 1st Division, formed by their 4 best battleships, the 2nd Division, the old irons of the 3rd Division (the obsolete battleships Nicola I, Apraxin, Seniavin, Usciakoff), some good cruisers, and several auxiliary ships (4 transports, two tugboats and two hospital ships); the few torpedo boats are scattered here and there with functions of escort, liaison and possible transfer of officers. The Explorers Squadron completes the Russian forces.

The Japanese ships under the command of Admiral Togo hinge on four modern battleships (Mikasa, Shikishima,

La flotta russa del Pacifico, dopo un incredibile viaggio che l'ha portata da San Pietroburgo all'Estremo Oriente tenta di forzare il canale di Tsushima, isola posta tra il Giappone e la Corea, strada obbligata per portarsi a Vladivostok, ultima fortezza russa dopo la caduta di Port Arthur. Le navi russe, aldilà dell'inferiorità tecnologica, sono in pessime condizioni per il lungo viaggio e con equipaggi stanchi e demoralizzati. Per contro, i giapponesi hanno avuto tutto il tempo per prepararsi a questo scontro che avviene a casa loro con la buona prospettiva di poterla spuntare.

Forze in campo

La squadra russa è composta dalla 1a Divisione, formata dalle loro 4 migliori corazzate, dalla 2a Divisione, dai vecchi ferri da stiro della 3a Divisione (le obsolete corazzate Nicola I, Apraxin, Seniavin, Usciakoff), da alcuni buoni incrociatori, e da diverse navi ausiliarie (4 trasporti, due rimorchiatori e due navi ospedale); le poche torpediniere-siluranti sono sparpagliate di qua e là con funzioni di scorta, di collegamento e di eventuale trasferimento degli ufficiali. La Squadra Esploratori completa le forze russe.

Le navi giapponesi sotto il comando dell'Ammiraglio Togo fanno perno su quattro corazzate moderne (Mikasa, Shiki-

▲ Admiral Tōgō Heihachirō on the bridge of the Battleship Mikasa.

 Russian Destroyer 1905 (3,5ton. 26 knots crew 60 armament : 1 75mm 5 47mm 2 torpedo)
Torpediniere russe 1905 (3,5 ton. 6 nodi equipaggio 60, armamento : 1 75mm 5 47mm 2 torpedo)

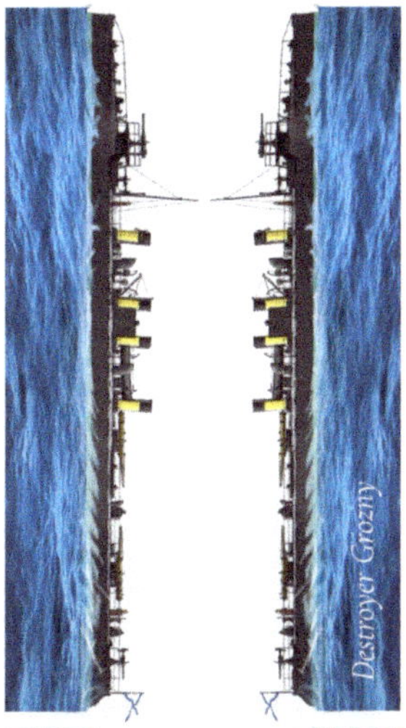

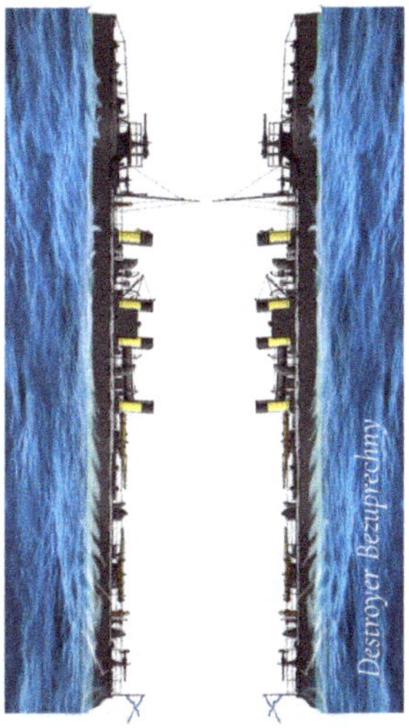

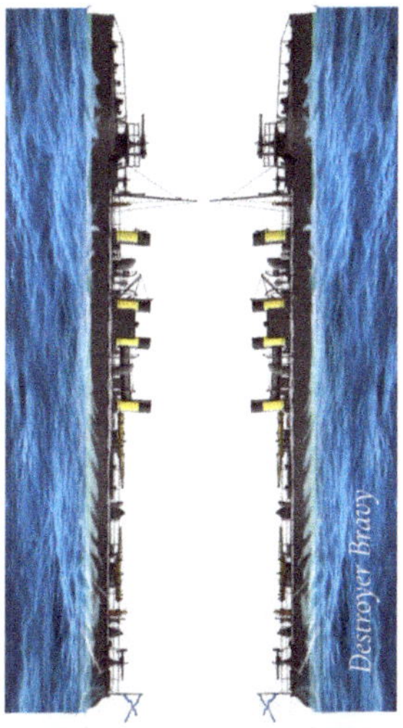

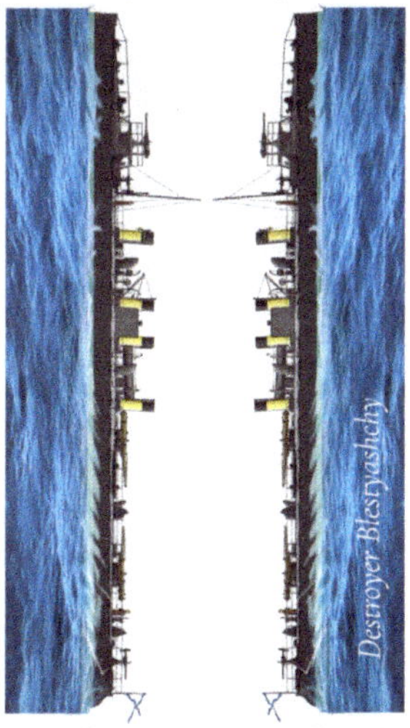

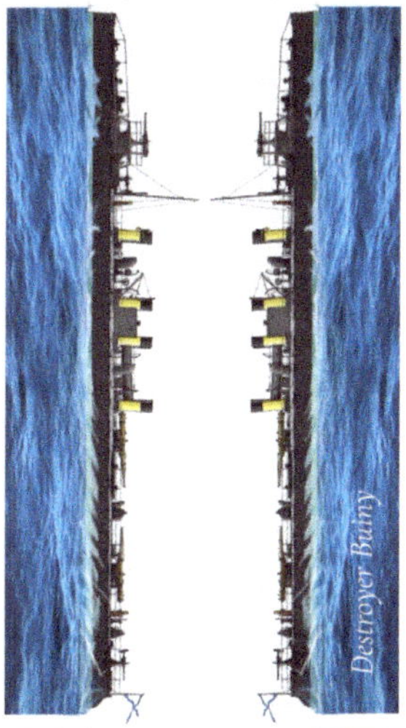

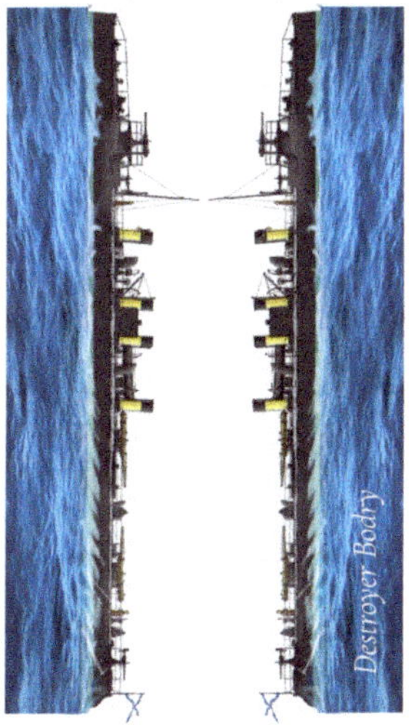

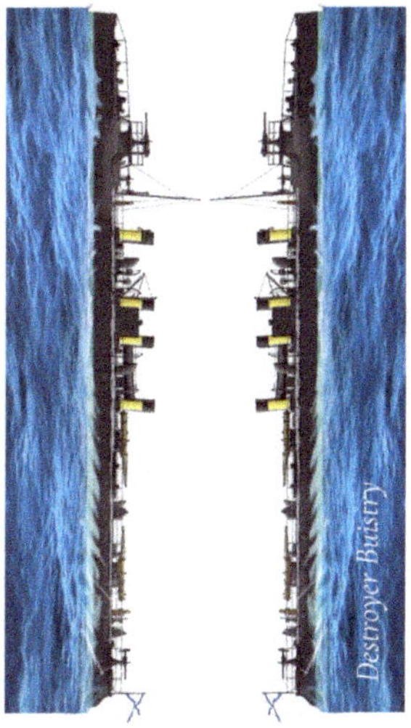

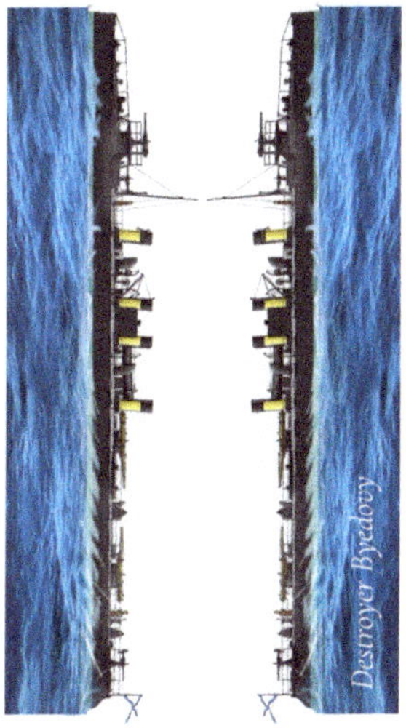

- Destroyer Grozny
- Destroyer Bezupreciny
- Destroyer Bratiy
- Destroyer Gromky
- Destroyer Blestyashchy
- Destroyer Boiny
- Destroyer Bodry
- Destroyer Buisiry
- Destroyer Byedoiy

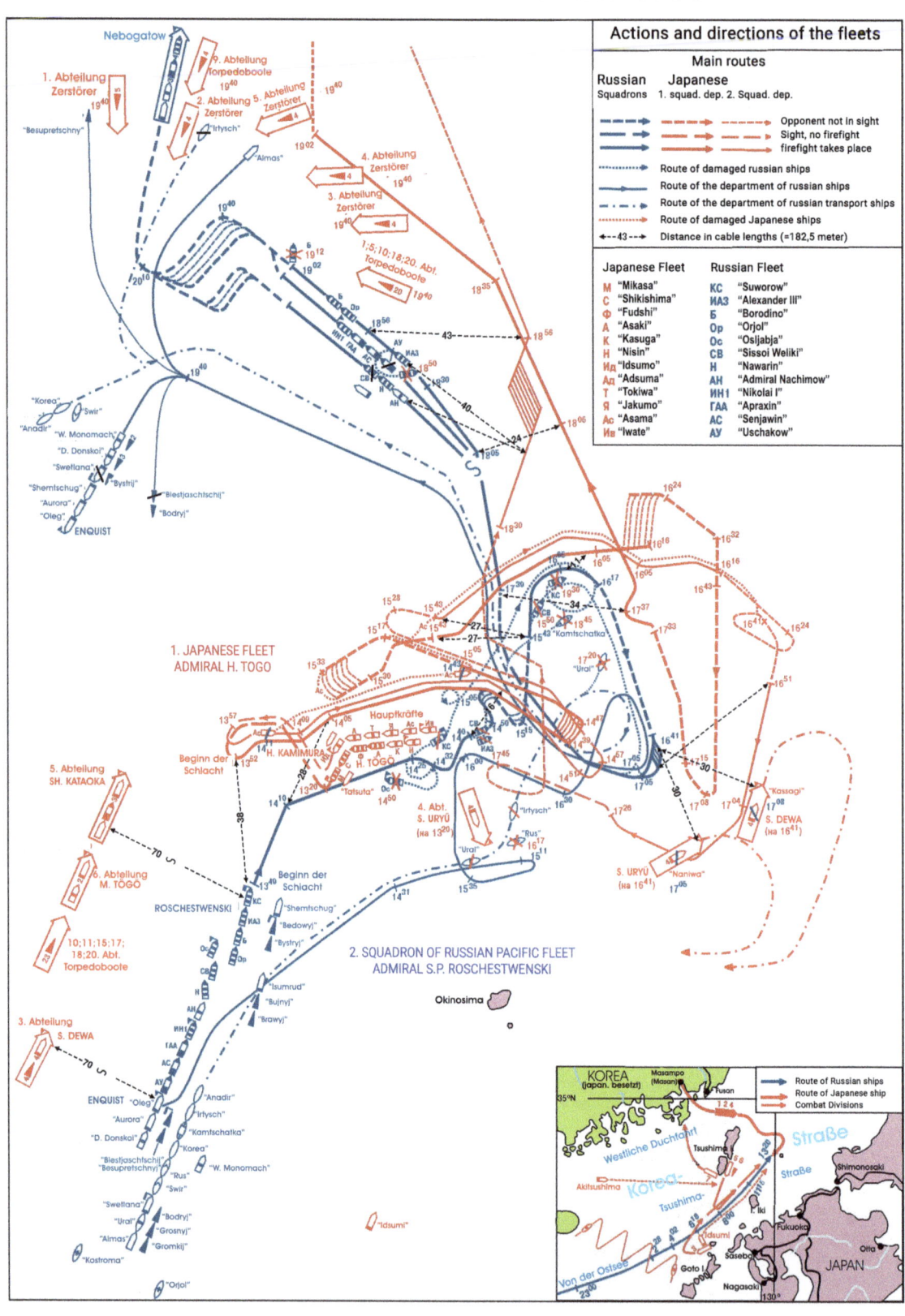

1904-1905 RUSSO-JAPAN WAR - RUSSIAN ARMY - 1904-1905 GUERRA RUSSO GIAPPONESE - ESERCITO RUSSO

Asahi and Fuji), the two modern armoured cruisers Kasuga and Nisshin designed in Italy. Other armored cruisers, an old ex-Chinese battleship (Chin Yuen), and a large number of torpedo boat- torpedo boat flotillas and many fighters that had already proved valuable for the battle of Port Arthur. The Russians sailed lined up on two columns: the 1st and 2nd divisions on the right, the direction of probable origin of the enemy, the other ships on the left. The Japanese squadron has the division of scouts lined up in a rake in front of the battle squadron, which proceeds in a row with the battleship division at the head and the armoured cruisers to follow. Contact between the two squads takes place at approximately 13:00: the Japanese scouts transmit their enemy's position and formation and retreat to their battleships to avoid ending up under fire from the enemy's big guns.

The beginning of the battle
Both fleets make a series of strategic mistakes during the approach. The Russians are now the protagonists of an incredible manoeuvring error, which, due to a series of unfortunate coincidences, leads them to try to assume a useful combat formation and instead end up returning to the same starting position... The Japanese also commit a serious imprudence of the same species. Both forces will not take advantage of these first mistakes.

The battle
Ballistic contact between the two teams takes place around 14:10, with the Japanese in an extremely advantageous position. However, the first saves are incredibly favourable to the Russians: the old irons do their duty, hitting the enemy armored cruisers several times at the tail of the Japanese formation and even damaging the flagship Mikasa, while Togo is miraculously unharmed. Twenty minutes later the situation turns upside down. The Suvoroff is hit repeatedly and at around 14:45 it is practically out of action. The Osliabia undergoes the same treatment as the Russian flagship and drops dead at 15:05.
The Russians at this point are about to parade aft to the Japanese, who have overtaken them, but Togo with skilful maneuvers cuts the Russians off again, forcing them into battle. The area of the fight is now darkened by smoke, and torpedo boats and light fighters take advantage of it to get into action. Towards 18:00 the shooting of the big guns resumed: the Japanese continued to concentrate their fire, in succession, causing a long series of casualties in the Russian ranks: first it was the Alexander III which sank at 18:55, then it was the turn of the Borodino which sank at 19:10, finally the Suvoroff was found and sunk at 19:20.
With the arrival of darkness, the commander of the old battleships escaped from the 3rd Division, Admiral Ne-

shima, Asahi e Fuji), i due moderni incrociatori corazzati Kasuga e Nisshin progettati in Italia. Altri incrociatori corazzati, una vecchia corazzata ex-cinese (Chin Yuen), e una nutrita serie di flottiglie di torpediniere-siluranti e molti caccia che si erano dimostrati già preziosi per la battaglia di Port Arthur. I russi navigano schierati su due colonne: la 1a e la 2a divisione a destra, la direzione di probabile provenienza del nemico, le altre navi a sinistra. La squadra giapponese ha la divisione di esploratori schierata a rastrello davanti alla squadra da battaglia, che procede in linea di fila con la divisione delle corazzate in testa e gli incrociatori corazzati a seguire. Il contatto tra le due squadre avviene circa alle 13:00: gli esploratori giapponesi trasmettono posizione e formazione del nemico e si ritirano verso le proprie corazzate per evitare di finire sotto il tiro dei grossi calibri nemici.

L'inizio della battaglia
Entrambe le flotte commettono una serie di errori strategici durante l'approccio di avvicinamento. I russi sono ora protagonisti di un incredibile errore di manovra, che per una serie di coincidenze sfortunate li porta a tentare di assumere una formazione utile al combattimento e finiscono invece per rimettersi nella stessa posizione di partenza... Anche i giapponesi commettono una grave imprudenza della stessa specie. Entrambe le forze non approfitteranno di questi primi errori.

Il combattimento
Il contatto balistico tra le due squadre avviene intorno alle 14:10, con i giapponesi in posizione estremamente vantaggiosa. Tuttavia, le prime salve sono incredibilmente favorevoli ai russi: i vecchi ferri da stiro fanno il loro dovere, centrando a più riprese gli incrociatori corazzati nemici, in coda alla formazione giapponese, e danneggiano persino l'ammiraglia Mikasa, e Togo è miracolosamente illeso. Venti minuti dopo la situazione si capovolge. la Suvoroff è colpita ripetutamente e attorno alle 14:45 è praticamente fuori combattimento. l'Osliabia subisce lo stesso trattamento dell'ammiraglia russa e cola a picco alle 15:05.
I russi a questo punto stanno per sfilare di poppa ai giapponesi, che li hanno sopravanzati, ma Togo con abili manovre taglia nuovamente la rotta ai russi, costringendoli alla battaglia. La zona dello scontro è ormai oscurata dal fumo, ne approfittano le torpediniere e i caccia leggeri per entrare in azione. Verso le 18.00 riprende il tiro dei grossi calibri: i giapponesi continuano a concentrare il fuoco, in successione, provocando una lunga serie di vittime nelle fila russe: prima è la Alexander III che affonderà alle 18:55, poi è la volta della Borodino che affonda alle 19:10, infine la Suvoroff è scovata ed affondata alle 19:20.
Con l'arrivo dell'oscurità, il comandante delle vecchi corazzate scampate della 3a divisione, ammiraglio Nebo-

Tsushima battle: Fires and explosions
Battaglia di Tsushima fuoco ed esplosioni

boghatoff, desperately orders to continue north, initially defending himself successfully from the attack of enemy torpedoes. At dawn on 28 May, the situation was as follows: the old and obsolete irons, although with varying degrees of damage, were still together, the other ships were either lost or sunk. Reaching the Japanese battleships, much faster and with a higher range of cannons, Admiral Neboghatoff made the only logical choice, the surrender of his units.

The balance of the two days is a Waterloo for the Russians: of the 7 Russian battleships employed, 6 were sunk (Osliabia, Suvaroff, Alexander III, Borodino, Sissoi Veliky and Navarin) and one captured (Orel); of the 4 old second class battleships, 1 was sunk (Usciakoff) and the others captured (Nicola I, Apraxin, Seniavin). All 3 Russian armored cruisers ended up at the bottom of the sea. Of the 6 protected cruisers only one managed to reach the Russian base. Others were shamefully interned in the Philippines (Aurora, Oleg, Jemciug). With the ships the Russians also lost 5,000 men and another 7,000 ended up as prisoners. The Japanese complained about 116 dead and 558 wounded and only three torpedoes.

The real key to the defeat appeared in all its evidence from the posthumous analysis of the clash and was largely attributable to the decidedly better quality of their Japanese ships, but above all of the really bad Russian and non-Russian bullets, mind the artillerymen: a destroyer was hit 32 times but nevertheless returned to base with only one wounded on board; also the flagship of Togo, the Mikasa, which took about 20 shots of 305 and 254mm, with the result of complaining damage only to a 305 piece of the bow tower that was knocked out...

ghatoff, ordina disperatamente di proseguire verso nord, difendendosi inizialmente con successo dall'attacco delle siluranti nemiche. All'alba del 28 maggio la situazione è la seguente: i vecchi e obsoleti ferri da stiro, benché con danni di varia entità, sono ancora insieme, le altre navi sono disperse o affondate. Raggiunti dalle navi da battaglia giapponesi, decisamente più veloci e con superiore portata dei cannoni inducono, l'Ammiraglio Neboghatoff a fare l'unica scelta logica, la resa delle sue unità.

Il bilancio delle due giornate è una Waterloo per i russi: delle 7 corazzate russe impiegate, 6 sono state affondate (Osliabia, Suvaroff, Alexander III, Borodino, Sissoi Veliky e Navarin) ed una catturata (Orel); delle 4 vecchie corazzate di seconda classe, 1 fu affondata (Usciakoff) e le altre catturate (Nicola I, Apraxin, Seniavin). Tutti e 3 gli incrociatori corazzati russi sono finiti in fondo al mare. Dei 6 incrociatori protetti uno solo è riuscito a raggiungere la base russa. Altri si sono fatti vergognosamente internare nelle Filippine (Aurora, Oleg, Jemciug). Con le navi i russi hanno perso anche 5.000 uomini e altri 7.000 finiti prigionieri. I giapponesi lamentarono 116 morti e 558 feriti e solo tre siluranti.

La vera chiave della disfatta apparve in tutta la sua evidenza dall'analisi postuma dello scontro e fu imputabile in gran parte alla decisamente migliore qualità delle loro navi giapponesi, ma soprattutto di quelle veramente pessime dei proiettili russi e non, si badi bene degli artiglieri: un cacciatorpediniere, venne colpito ben 32 volte ma ciononostante rientrò alla base con un solo ferito a bordo; anche la ammiraglia di Togo, la Mikasa, che incassò circa 20 colpi da 305 e 254mm, col risultato di lamentare danni solo ad un pezzo da 305 della torre prodiera che fu messo fuori uso...

PAPER BATTLE&DIORAMAS PUBLISHED AND IN WORKING

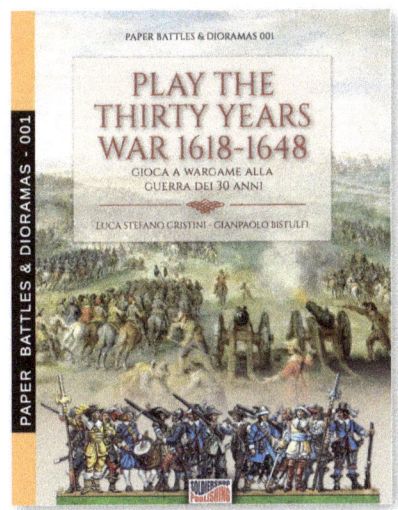
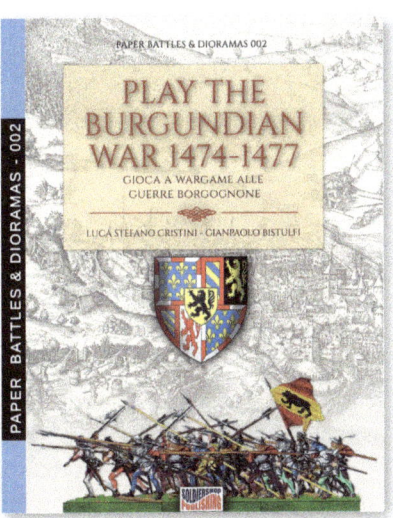
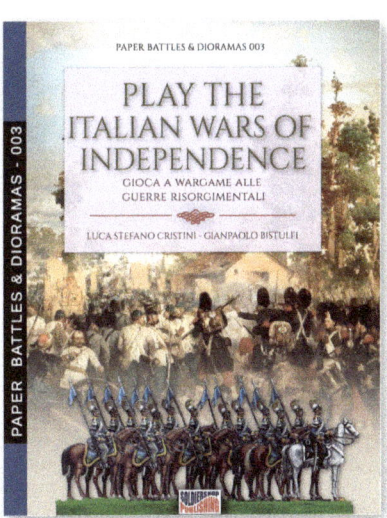
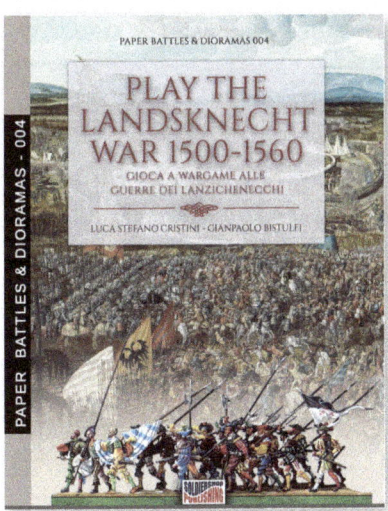
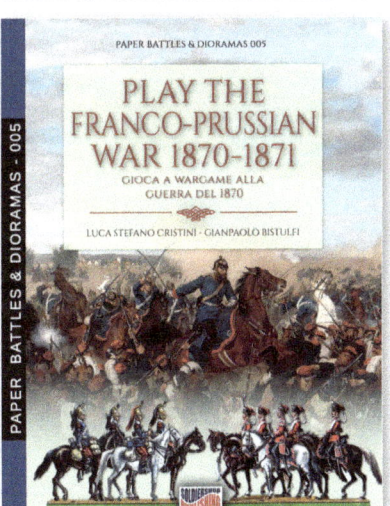
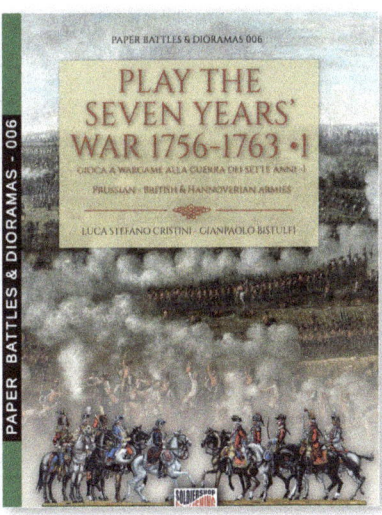
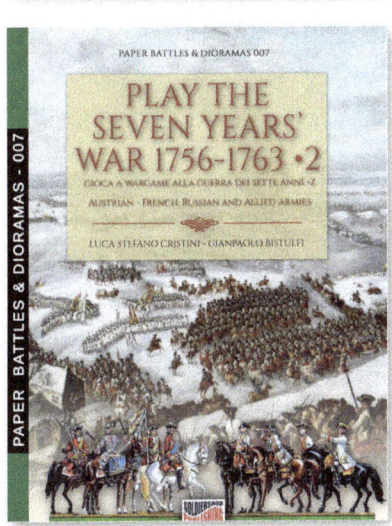
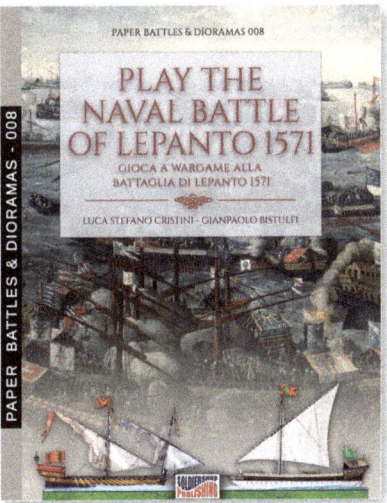
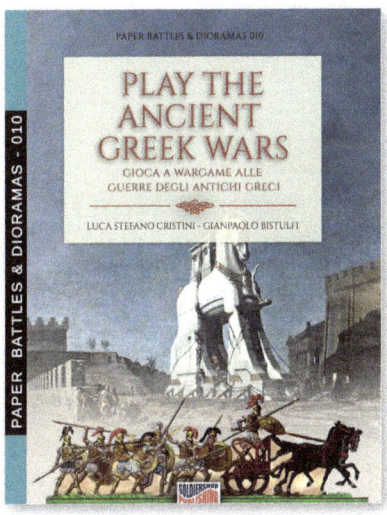

www.ingramcontent.com/pod-product-compliance
Ingram Content Group UK Ltd.
Pitfield, Milton Keynes, MK11 3LW, UK
UKHW060214240426
12048UKWH00031BB/1718